MY ISRAEL
Seventy Faces of the Land

Nechemia (Chemi) J. Peres

Ilan Greenfield

Copyright © Nechemia (Chemi) J. Peres
Jerusalem 2023/5783

All rights reserved. No part of this publication may be translated, reproduced, stored in a retrieval system or transmitted, in any form or by any means, electronic, mechanical, photocopying, recording or otherwise, without express written permission from the publishers.

Excerpt from "Response to an Italian Captain" by Natan Alterman translated from the Hebrew by Marie Syrkin, *Blessed Is the Match: The Story of Jewish Resistance* (Philadelphia: The Jewish Publication Society, 1947). Used by permission.

Cover photo: Itai Bardov
Cover and Design: Studio Rami&Jaki

ISBN: 978-965-7023-35-8

1 3 5 7 9 8 6 4 2

Gefen Publishing House Ltd.	Gefen Books
6 Hatzvi Street	c/o Baker & Taylor Publisher Services
Jerusalem 9438614,	30 Amberwood Parkway
Israel	Ashland, Ohio 44805
972-2-538-0247	516-593-1234
orders@gefenpublishing.com	orders@gefenpublishing.com

www.gefenpublishing.com

Printed in Israel
Library of Congress Control Number: 2022916816

To my parents, Sonia and Shimon, who came to Israel before there was a state

And to my family: Gila, Nadav, Guy, Yael, Noam, Tamar, and Zohar

Contents

Preface – Chemi Peres	ix
Letter from the Publisher – Ilan Greenfield	xi

Part I Zionist History: Sacrifice for the Homeland

Becoming Israeli at Mount Herzl – Eli Beer	2
Mount Herzl: A National and Personal Journey – Ziv Shilon	4
Transcending Limits at Mount Herzl – Itai Cohen	7
Finding My Israeli Identity at the President's Residence – Brigadier General (Ret.) Hasson Hasson	10
The Atlit Immigrant Detention Camp – Murray Greenfield, as told to Elli Wohlgelernter	13
The Zionist Dream in Yarkona and Ramot Hashavim – Jonathan Kolber	16
Remembering Heroes at Exodus Memorial Garden – Sharon Harel-Cohen	20
The Abandoned Boat at Dor Beach – Kira Radinsky	22
The Night Sky in the Valley of the Cross – Gideon Argov	25
The Revolution Starts in Moshav Beit Zayits – Lili Ben-Ami	27
Kibbutz Kfar Etzion Full of Life – Achiya Klein	30
Roots at the Military Cemetery in Kibbutz Kiryat Anavim – Nadav Zafrir	33
The Olive Trees at Kibbutz Revivim – Pierre Besnainou	36
The Circle of Moshav Nahalal – Ayelet Nahmias-Verbin	38
The Legacy of Mitzpe Yair, Kibbutz Ramat Rachel – Jossef Avi Yair "Jucha" Engel	41
In the Footsteps of Warriors at Amir Trail – Lieutenant General Gadi Eizenkot	45
A Sense of Mission at Nabi Samuel: Samuel's Tomb – Miriam Peretz	47

Photo: Gil Shwed

Part II Nature: The Land of Milk and Honey

The Brilliant Scars of Makhtesh Ramon – Dan Ariely	50
Finding Clarity at Hod Akev – Stav Shaffir	53
Belonging in the Desert: Yeruham – Tal Ohana	56
Big Dreams at the Fountain of Youth Ranch – Tchia Efron Klinger	58
The Desert Is Blooming in Neot Hovav – Chen Lichtenstein	60
Finding Home at the Dead Sea – Marcelle Machluf	62
Kalia: A Hopeful Landscape – Sivan Yaari	64
Tel Beit Shemesh: Beit Shemesh for All – Aliza Bloch	66
Serving My Country in Re'ut – Brigadier General (Ret.) Dani Harari	69
Always on the Way to Arsuf Beach – Adi Altschuler	72
Kfar Malal and the Long-Gone Casuarina Trees – Gilad Sharon	74
Peace on Mount Tavor – Ido Schoenberg and Phyllis Gotlib	77

Part III Social Equality: Coexistence and Unity

The Music of Coexistence in Akko – Ofra Strauss	81
Finding Strength Together in Haifa – Imad Telhami	84
Growing Community at Bustan Thom (Thom's Orchard) – Noam Gershony	89
Higher High Tech on Mount Carmel – Maysa Halabi Alshekh	92
Encounters, Connections, and Opportunities at Beit Harishonot – Hana Rado	97
Opportunity at Reichman University (IDC Herzliya) – Joey Low	99
A Message of Unity from Kiryat Adam, Lod – Eytan Stibbe	101
An Ethiopian Story in Gedera – Yuvi Tashome-Katz	104
The Shalva National Center: A Global Model of Inclusion – Kalman Samuels	106
Together at ANU – Museum of the Jewish People – Irina Nevzlin	110
Ben Gurion Airport: Portal to the Homeland – Sivan Rahav-Meir	114

Part IV Spirituality: History of the Jewish People

The Western Wall in the Holy City of Jerusalem – Rabbi Shmuel Rabinovitch	119
Praying for Clarity Together at the Kotel – Dr. Yael Gold-Zamir	122
The Outlook from Ma'alot Benny ("Benny's Ascent") – Rabbi Binyamin Lau	125
Life and Abyss at the Foundation Stone, Temple Mount – Rabbi Mordechai Bar-Or	127
The Binding of Isaac: A True Story, or Not – Lior Suchard	131
Dreaming at the Austrian Hospice – Sharonna Karni Cohen	134
The Forest of the Martyrs, Where Every Person Has a Tree – Tamara Kolitz	136

Part V Culture and Leisure: Life in Israel

Masada and My Sunrise Concerts – David Broza	141
A Dose of Optimism at Tmol Shilshom – Shira Rivelis	144
The Bustle of Jerusalem's Central Bus Station – Dr. Avital Beck	147
At Home on Metzitzim Beach, Tel Aviv – Inbal Arieli	149
Lifelong Friendship on the Tel Aviv Beach – Orit Gadiesh	151
Coming Alive at Habima National Theater – Aki Avni	154
Nazareth Market: The Pearl of Nazareth – Julia Zaher	156
Kinneret Cemetery: In Loving Memory of Guy Peres – Chemi Peres	158

Part VI Education and Sports: Excellence of the Mind and Body

Vitality at the Technion – Avichai (Avi) Kremer	163
The Pioneering Spirit at the Faculty of Biomedical Engineering, the Technion – Shulamit Levenberg	166
The Best of Israel at the Wingate Institute – Arik Ze'evi	169
Multidisciplinary Diversity at Tel Aviv University – Ronit Satchi-Fainaro	172
The Fight for Excellence at Maccabi Tel Aviv – Yael Arad	175
The Vision at ORT School for Science and Engineering, Lod – Shirin Natour-Hafi	178
Boosting High Tech at Hebrew University of Jerusalem – Ruth Polachek	180
Inspiration at Hama'alot Theater, Mount Scopus – Inbar Harush Gity	184

Part VII Technology, Innovation, and Entrepreneurship: The Innovation Nation

Probing the Stars at Mitzpe Ramon Astronomical Observation Center – Inbal (Biran) Kreiss	188
Raising the Scientific Bar in Beer Sheva – Orna Berry	191
Old Meets New at First Station – Hillel Fuld	193
Building Bridges at KamaTech Innovation Center, Bnei Brak – Moshe Friedman	197
Tel Aviv: A Concept City – Gil Shwed	201
My Corner of Rothschild Boulevard, Tel Aviv – Adi Soffer Teeni	203
Innovation in Tel Aviv – Itay Pincas	206
The Peres Center for Peace and Innovation – Chemi Peres	208
Acknowledgments – Chemi Peres and Ilan Greenfield	213
Index of Contributors	215
About the Compiler – Chemi Peres	217
About the Compiler – Ilan Greenfield	219

Photo: Yoram Reshef

Chemi Peres

Preface

Israel was born out of a great vision. It was built by dreamers and pioneers who believed they could shape a new future for our people.

They came from many countries around the world, speaking many languages, bringing with them different cultures and experiences. Many of them left their homes and families behind them, hoping to reunite one day in our homeland.

It is a story of human spirit. When the first newcomers made aliyah, they found a small, dry piece of land. A land with swamps in the north and desert in the south. It was almost impossible to grow crops on this depleted soil. We had neither mountains nor wide rivers that could slow down potential invaders. There was no shelter to safeguard us from a surrounding hostile neighborhood. We were blessed with no natural resources.

The first settlers knew they could only rely on hard work, creativity, and resiliency. Over time, they managed to dry up the swamps in the north and make the desert bloom.

They built the beautiful country we all love so much.

In the brief history of the State of Israel, what we have achieved collectively as a people exceeds the brightest dreams of our founding fathers, perhaps beyond their imagination.

The story of Israel is a story of our people. It is a story of a diversified society that continues to thrive and grow strong, from one generation to another.

This book is a journey of discovery, designed to learn about Israel through the eyes of people we have met over the years – people whose hard work and dreams we learned to respect. It all started with a childhood friend, Ilan Greenfield, who became a companion of mine for this journey. Ilan agreed to work with me on publishing this book, and I am grateful for his dedication and friendship.

We decided to invite some seventy individuals, women and men from all walks of life, to share with us their own individual perspectives on what they consider to be "My Israel."

We asked each of them to choose one place that represents for them the essence of being an Israeli and share with us why they picked that specific location. The result of their work is put forward in this book, showing the magic of a colorful landscape.

We hope this project will give you an opportunity to meet and learn about the people participating in this volume and to be exposed to some of the most beautiful and interesting spots in Israel, whether you are seeing them for the first time or getting reacquainted through different lenses.

As participants in this journey of discovery, Ilan's father and I chose our own locations to be included in the beautiful puzzle. Initially, I chose to write about the Peres Center for Peace and Innovation in Jaffa. My father, Shimon Peres, who served as Israel's ninth president and its eighth prime minister, landed in the port of Old Jaffa in 1934, before we had our state, accompanied by his brother and mother.

Sixty-two years later, in 1996, he founded the Peres Center for Peace and Innovation, later establishing its offices in a beautiful building in the heart of Jaffa's Ajami neighborhood. He spent the last years of his life working at the Peres Center. The story of Israel and his forward-looking legacy are presented to the public in this place, working to grow our country strong while achieving long-lasting peace in our region.

During our work compiling this book, collecting writers and landscapes, on March 16, 2022, my wife Gila and I tragically lost our middle son Guy, brother to Nadav and Yael. Guy was just thirty-three years old when he left us. We were all shocked and devastated by his unexpected and untimely passing due to sudden heart failure. I decided to add another chapter about the beautiful old cemetery on the shores of the Sea of Galilee, dedicated in loving memory to Guy.

That became my Israel.

Ilan Greenfield

Letter from the Publisher

וְיֹתֵר מֵהֵמָּה, בְּנִי הִזָּהֵר: עֲשׂוֹת סְפָרִים הַרְבֵּה אֵין קֵץ, וְלַהַג הַרְבֵּה יְגִעַת בָּשָׂר.

קהלת יב, יב

More than this, my child, beware of making too many books; critique without end makes the flesh weary. *Ecclesiastes 12:12*

After more than forty years of being a publisher, one must stop and think – am I publishing yet another book just because this is my habit? Is there added value to this book? Will the world be a better place once this book is published?

I thank the Creator for the gift He gave me. The gift of loving books, and especially the gift of being able to publish books, each one a memorable creation that I believe will illuminate the world by spreading knowledge and enhancing the lives of all who read it.

Several years ago, I compiled and published *My Jerusalem*, with over fifty essays by a select group of individuals from all over the world. Each wrote what the words "My Jerusalem" meant to them. This was not a historical book but a personal one, an inside view from the perspective of those who know and love the city, reflecting what Jerusalem really is.

My Jerusalem included a piece by the late Shimon Peres, former Prime Minister and President of Israel. When I presented a copy of the published book to Chemi Peres so he could enjoy his father's essay, he loved the book and suggested that we publish *My Israel*.

His concept was a unique and revolutionary take on a travel guide. This would not be an ordinary guidebook describing the historical sites in our beautiful country, but rather a set of personal narratives with seventy essays, each by an extraordinary, accomplished individual from all walks of life – an entrepreneur, a singer, an athlete, and many other innovative and productive citizens of this land we love. Each contributor decided which site in Israel they wanted to show the world. Each and every one of these sites holds special meaning for our contributors, who represent the full spectrum of Israeli society, including Jews of all streams, Christians, Muslims, and Druze. The one common denominator to all these writers is their love for Israel.

The collaboration with my friend of many years, Chemi, to produce *My Israel* is certainly one of the highlights of my four decades of publishing.

I do hope that whether at home or on your next trip to Israel, you will enjoy the book and take advantage of the many insider perspectives presented here to enhance your connection to Israel, the Holy Land.

PART I

ZIONIST HISTORY
Sacrifice for the Homeland

Photo: Amit Gabay-Murvitz

Eli Beer is president and founder of United Hatzalah of Israel, whose model of using community-based emergency medical responders has been implemented in twenty-one countries and has resulted in hundreds of thousands of lives being saved. He has received numerous awards.

Eli Beer

Becoming Israeli at Mount Herzl

Mount Herzl is where I became an Israeli. I was born into an ultra-Orthodox Jewish family from the United States. My parents, Gavriel, of blessed memory, and Chaya Beer, may she live a long life, loved the Land of Israel, but Zionism was not their ideology. My father's family came to New York from Galicia, the cradle of the Chassidic movement. My mother's family immigrated from Germany to the Big Apple. As newlyweds, they dreamed of making aliyah to Israel to fulfill the mitzvah of settling the Holy Land. After the Six-Day War, when Israel's decisive victory inspired admiration around the world and particularly among Jews, they shuttered their real estate and insurance businesses in the United States and moved to Israel with my six brothers and sisters.

I was born in Bayit VeGan – a warm, close-knit neighborhood in Jerusalem, founded by leaders of the ultra-Orthodox movement Poalei Agudat Yisrael – but I was no Israeli by birth. At home, we spoke English, and we were taught to love Israel as the Holy Land that was promised to our forefathers. But at the *cheder* (religious elementary school) I attended, it was very much like *Shtisel*, and we were forbidden from mentioning the names of the Zionist leaders who established the state. Herzl, Weizmann, Ben-Gurion, Jabotinsky? These individuals and the various streams of Zionism were not part of the ultra-Orthodox curriculum.

Across from the neighborhood where I grew up stands one of the most beautiful places I've ever known – Mount Herzl. As a curious, mischievous boy, I frequently crossed the broad width of Herzl Avenue and passed through a gate that led to an imposing cypress forest. I was particularly fond of one of the hills. I used to climb up to the top, lie on my back, and roll down the cropped, fragrant grass. I spent many long hours there. As a child, I didn't pay much attention to the marble tombstones, the rectangular stone plots, and the memorials that surrounded me. But eventually, I began to read the words on the stones.

Photo: Shiran Halimi

At age ten, I was well aware of what a grave meant. But while wandering among them, I noticed something very shocking. This was a cemetery for young people! Most of the soldiers buried there were in their late teens. By reading the headstones, I was able to glean information on the reasons for their death. I learned about Israel's wars and military operations, about the tragedy and grief that are part of our everyday lives here in Israel. I discovered the memorials for brave Jewish soldiers who had fought in the two World Wars, and those who had battled in Eretz Yisrael before the establishment of the state and the IDF. I found the plot reserved for soldiers whose bodies were never found.

At home, I began to read about the wars and military operations that I remembered from the brave soldiers' graves. On my own, I studied the actions of the nation's leaders who are buried under the marble tombstones. This new information changed everything I knew about our life here in Eretz Yisrael.

At fifteen, I discovered my purpose in life: to fight death and save lives. I began to volunteer as a first responder on an ambulance. Often, we simply arrived too late. I realized that the time for providing medical treatment had to be shortened, and I set out to do just that.

One of the things that most influenced me during my visits to Mount Herzl was the multicultural mosaic created by the names of the fallen. Diaspora names and Israeli names. Ashkenazi, Sephardi, and Hebraicized names. The names are carved into identical stone tablets that were manufactured in the early days of the state as part of the IDF's melting pot approach.

But the uniformity of the tablets cannot erase the diversity of the fallen, and this awareness guided me in creating the United Hatzalah emergency medical response organization. Our volunteers are religious and secular, Ashkenazi and Sephardi, Jews, Christians, and Muslims, all working together. For many of them, this volunteer service is a portal to the world of the other. A Jewish settler volunteer from East Jerusalem enters the home of a neighboring Arab family and provides medical treatment – and vice versa. An ultra-Orthodox volunteer from Bnei Brak helps a secular individual from Tel Aviv. Since the day we established the organization, we've treated six million men and women in Israel.

I am certain that my father is looking down on me from above with pride in this effort. To me it is the ultimate expression of Zionism. Its seeds were planted on Mount Herzl – the place where I became an Israeli.

Ziv Shilon

Mount Herzl: A National and Personal Journey

Ziv Shilon *is an entrepreneur and public speaker, named a Forbes 30 Under 30 up-and-coming leader. His left arm was amputated and his right severely injured during his service as an officer in the IDF's Givati Brigade. After rehabilitation, Ziv completed the Iron Man triathlon. He has received a medal of honor.*

Every nation has places that portray its roots and history and reflect the journey that shaped it. Similarly, every person has places particularly close to the heart that represent significant moments. Mount Herzl in Jerusalem is that place both for our nation and for myself personally.

Mount Herzl is named after Theodor Herzl, visionary of the Jewish state and founder of modern Zionism. In 1949, Herzl's remains were brought from Vienna per his wishes and reinterred on a mountain in Jerusalem, which was renamed in his honor. Located on the west side of Jerusalem, it hosts Israel's national cemetery, established in 1949 for soldiers who had fallen in and near Jerusalem during the country's War of Independence. Later that year, Israel's first government decided to turn the site into the National Military Cemetery, where key figures leading to the establishment of the State of Israel would also be buried.

The cemetery is divided into several sections, including Great Leaders of the Nation, where Israel's presidents, prime ministers, and Knesset speakers are laid to rest; Leaders of the World Zionist Organization, where presidents and chairmen of the World Zionist Organization are buried; and the National Military Cemetery. Yad Vashem World Holocaust Remembrance Center rests on the western slope of Mount Herzl, and together these sites encompass the Mount of Remembrance, which recognizes instrumental figures in the history of the Jewish people and the State of Israel over the past century.

Mount Herzl became a place of personal significance for me at the end of April 2008. A few weeks earlier, my combat unit had begun operating along the Gaza Strip, defending Israel's borders. On April 16, 2008, at six a.m., a cell of six Hamas terrorists approached the fence in an attempt to infiltrate Israel. Our unit, as part of the Zabar Infantry Battalion, was the first to respond. In the exchange of fire, two of my very best friends were killed: Sgt.

David Papian, who had made aliyah mainly to serve in the IDF, and Sgt. Matan Ovdati, who insisted on serving as a combat soldier despite having lost his father just a year and a half before his enlistment.

The next morning, my unit went to their funerals. I will never forget that day. It was an unusually cold day in Jerusalem; I was shaking. I could not stop thinking about the soldiers' last moments. My heart was broken, but I was unable to cry. It was the first time I had lost someone so close, people I had been with twenty-four seven. We had shared countless meaningful experiences: laughing, sweating, hurting, huddling close to keep warm, eating from the same plate – brothers in arms.

That was my initial experience of Mount Herzl as a personal place, the first time I stood in front of the graves and imagined familiar faces. As I arrived at my parents' home in Beer Sheva later that day, I collapsed in tears. A month later, I returned to Mount Herzl, this time by myself. I stood in front of David's grave and thought about our last moment together. From the cemetery, I walked to Yad Vashem, where I spent hours thinking. That afternoon, I decided I was going to be an officer in the IDF, carrying the Jewish torch, honoring those who were lost along the way and fulfilling the promise "Never again."

I served in the IDF for six years and led hundreds of commanders and soldiers in various combat operations. Unfortunately, I lost another close friend, Maj. Yochai Kalangel, who fell during an operation in the northern frontier. Yochai was buried on Mount Herzl, which gave the place an even larger place in my heart. On October 23, 2012, the last day of my duty as company commander, I was badly injured by an explosive device, which amputated my left arm and severely wounded the right one. Knowing that I had survived while my brothers had not been as lucky enabled me to put things in perspective. It kept me positive during my rehabilitation and drove me to live a life full of achievements, leading social change and giving to others as much as I can.

Mount Herzl is a place that demonstrates the special link between the visionaries, the leaders, and those who fought and lost their lives in the fight for Israel. It is a link that symbolizes our country's journey, which became forever intertwined with my own. May it lead us to a safe and prosperous peace

Itai Cohen

Transcending Limits at Mount Herzl

Mount Herzl in Jerusalem is the burial site of Benjamin Ze'ev (Theodor) Herzl, the spiritual father of the Jewish state and founder of modern Zionism, whose remains were brought to the State of Israel from Vienna, Austria, in 1949.

The hill is also the burial site of other national leaders, presidents, and prime ministers of the State of Israel. One portion of the hill is a military burial ground for soldiers who sacrificed their lives in Israel's wars.

Mount Herzl is very green, with many tall trees and abundant shade, shrubbery, and flowering plants. The flourishing greenery symbolizes growth – in our lives, and in the state given to us by Herzl, national leaders, and the fallen soldiers. Many cedar trees grow on Mount Herzl, recalling the cedars of Lebanon used by King Solomon to build the Temple in Jerusalem.

Herzl's grave stands at the top of the hill, overlooking Jerusalem. The tombstone is rectangular, smooth black stone, carved simply with the name Herzl. Each year, the official Independence Day ceremony of the State of Israel is held at this gravesite.

Mount Herzl is also the site of the Herzl Center for Zionist Studies of the World Zionist Federation and the Herzl Museum. The museum tells the story of the life of Herzl, the leader who dreamed big and transformed Zionism into a national, practical movement, envisioning the establishment of the national home for the Jewish people in the Land of Israel. Herzl was a well-known, successful journalist who covered the Dreyfus Affair in Paris. During the trial, he realized that despite Emancipation and the Jews' efforts to assimilate into general society, antisemitism was growing. He concluded that the Jews must return to their ancestral homeland and establish their own state like other peoples, where they would be able to live safely and prosper.

Itai Cohen is a tour guide at the Herzl Museum as a National Civil Service volunteer. He completed a year of study at the Ein Prat premilitary academy and plans to study geography and political science at Hebrew University. He lives in Jerusalem with a caregiver and maintains an independent lifestyle.

A selection of photos from Mount Herzl: the exhibition, the simulation of the Zionist Congress, the tombstone, and the memorial site for the Ethiopian community (photos courtesy of the Herzl Center)

The Herzl Center produces educational programs and activities related to Herzl and Zionism, organizes tours of Mount Herzl and the museum for groups from Israel and abroad, hosts lectures and conferences, and conducts research on Herzl's life and activities.

At the Herzl Museum, visitors enjoy an interactive audiovisual presentation in eight languages. They pass through rooms that describe the history, dress, objects, and culture of the time period through photos, video clips, and special effects. Visitors are guided through the museum by a dramatic film narrated by an actor playing Herzl. Through the actor's journey, the visitors get to know Herzl's life and personality. They learn about his unique character, his habits and thoughts, and the transformation he underwent from respected journalist to visionary of the Jewish state.

Each of the museum rooms represents a station in Herzl's life: a Paris street in the late nineteenth century; the conference hall at the Zionist Congress in Basel; and Herzl's original office with furnishings brought over from his home in Vienna, along with objects that belonged to him. In the last room, we see a film that compares Herzl's vision as described in his book *Altneuland* and the reality of life in the modern State of Israel.

Mount Herzl tells the story of the Jewish people, from the Exile through the beginnings of the Zionist movement until the establishment of the State of Israel and our life here today.

My name is Itai Cohen. I am twenty-one years old and from Kfar Adumim, a town on the road from Jerusalem to the Dead Sea. I have a degenerative muscle disease and use a wheelchair, so I was unable to serve in the army. Instead, I chose to serve my country as a National Civil Service volunteer at the Herzl Center. I will soon finish my second year of service as a tour guide for groups at the Herzl Museum. In addition, I conduct research on Herzl. This year, I received the President's Award of Excellence for my work in the National Civil Service program.

I recommend that every individual who loves Israel and wishes to learn more about this country begin with a tour of Mount Herzl as the starting point in fulfilling the vision of the establishment of the State of Israel.

Brigadier General (Ret.) Hasson Hasson

Finding My Israeli Identity at the President's Residence

Brigadier General (Ret.) Hasson Hasson, *a member of Israel's Druze community, served in the IDF for thirty-seven years as a decorated officer. He was Military Secretary to President Shimon Peres and President Reuven Rivlin. He is CEO of Carmelist and a partner in Takwin Venture Capital and the Nevatim Fund.*

I cannot think of a place more representative of Israeli identity than Beit Hanasi, the President's Residence in Jerusalem, a place that has been more than a home to me.

Throughout my life, together with my wife and children, I have collected and internalized a variety of Israeli identities: Druze, soldier, intelligence agent, IDF officer, businessman, and more. In every role, I have placed my principles and my Israeli identity above all else.

In my long tenure as military secretary, I had the privilege of serving the ninth president of the State of Israel, the late Shimon Peres, followed by President Reuven Rivlin. The special time I spent at Beit Hanasi was when all my identities merged into a unified whole.

The President's Residence, known in Hebrew as Beit Hanasi or Mishkan Hanasi, has been the official residence of the president of Israel since 1971. It is located in the Talbiya neighborhood of Jerusalem on a hill of modest elevation, chosen deliberately to symbolize the status of the president as an elected official, but never above the people.

Everything here conveys a sense of identity. The residential wing is adorned with artwork created by Jewish and Israeli artists. The greenery in the garden was carefully selected to represent Israel's characteristic flora, including olive trees, cypress, and oak trees. Every world leader visiting Beit Hanasi is invited to plant an olive tree in the fittingly named Peace Garden, a tradition that began with President Peres during the visit to Israel of Pope Benedict XVI.

Here in the home of Israel's first citizen, I witnessed the astonishing power of the State of Israel. No other country in the world has faced so many threats to its national security in such a short span of time. In just under seven decades, Israel has withstood seven all-out wars with its neighboring Arab states, three local wars in Gaza, two intifadas,

and countless covert operations. Surviving in the jungle that is the Middle East is a constant struggle, one that Israel deals with on a daily basis.

Throughout it all, Israel has managed to reach incredible technological heights. I once personally heard the president of the People's Republic of China speak in amazement about Israel's flourishing high-tech industry and the ingenious Israeli mind. This is a leader of over 1.4 billion people astounded by the feats of a country so small one can hardly see it on the world map.

I met many other world leaders and remarkable businesspeople who saw Israel as spearheading global innovation in the defense and civilian arenas alike. They all posed the same question: How? What is the secret of Israel's power?

The late President Peres used to say that the State of Israel was lucky to have been blessed with nothingness. This is a land with no natural resources such as gas, oil, gold, or even sufficient water supplies. Scarcity led our nation to develop unrivaled creativity, the only resource we had in abundance. Add to this our spiritual power, manifested in leading thinkers, writers, and academics, and an ever-present volunteer spirit. Thanks to these qualities, Israel continues to overcome any limitation, erasing the word *impossible* from the Israeli vocabulary.

At Beit Hanasi, I attended many meetings whose purpose was to strengthen our relations with our neighbors, from Egypt to Jordan, the Persian Gulf, and the Palestinians. In quiet humility, we strove to achieve true peace. President Peres taught me that acting in the best interest of one's nation can go hand in hand with respecting and admiring other nations. Working alongside him, I realized that the stronger Israel gets, the better it is for the entire Middle East. It is this kind of value-driven leadership that has made Israeli leaders such as Shimon Peres so highly esteemed across the world.

My time at Beit Hanasi taught me that preserving our values and traditions is no contradiction to being open-minded and achieving technological breakthroughs. We are the connecting link between the glorious past and the future. It is our responsibility to preserve this link and to make sure the future is no less glorious.

Every day, I strive to put what I learned at Beit Hanasi into action with NGOs such as Coexistence and Israelis Against Racism that work to create unity between all groups of Israeli society, in addition to supporting families of fallen, kidnapped, and missing soldiers. I watch eagerly as the vision becomes a reality, and as our neighbors gradually understand that in every sense, from strategy to security, statehood, economy, and education, Israel is an important part of the world's solution.

Murray Greenfield, as told to Elli Wohlgelernter

The Atlit Immigrant Detention Camp

I did not have a Zionist upbringing and never had a longing to go help create a new country for the Jews. Yiddish was my mother tongue, New York Jew was my identity, and I was just happy to be alive in December 1946 after serving three years in the Merchant Marines during World War II.

But everything changed one Shabbat morning, when I found myself sitting in the back pews of the White Shul in Far Rockaway, New York, whispering with my buddies during services. We were discussing training during the war, and I told them, "I was on ships. I didn't like it, but I served on ships." And one of the fellas said, "They could use guys like you." He gave me the phone number to call, and that's how I got involved.

Our assignment was crazy: sail to Europe on broken-down ships, pick up Jewish Holocaust survivors who had somehow found their way to a port city on the Mediterranean Sea, and smuggle them to Palestine under the nose of the British. It was top secret, because the British had created a blockade to thwart the effort, declaring such immigration illegal. Beginning with the issuance of the White Paper in 1939 that closed off entry for Jews, any illegal ship en route to Palestine was stopped and taken over by the British.

A few thousand Jews fleeing Nazism made it past the blockade, but many more were captured and interned either in Cyprus or at the Atlit Detention Camp, a former military camp on the Mediterranean coast that the British converted to serve as a confinement camp for "illegal" refugees.

Murray Greenfield was a founder of the Association of Americans and Canadians in Israel, a representative of the American Association for Ethiopian Jews, an art dealer, and founder of Gefen Publishing House in Jerusalem. He is the author of The Jews' Secret Fleet. He lives in Tel Aviv, and his twenty great-grandchildren all live in Israel.

The Jews fought back. On the night of October 9–10, 1945, the Palmach – the Special Forces unit of the Haganah – broke into Atlit and freed 208 prisoners in a daring raid that caused the British to close the camp. Afterwards, between 1946 and 1949, Holocaust survivors and other Jews arrested for illegally trying to enter Palestine were sent mainly to the camp in Cyprus.

My ship, the *Hatikvah*, which was built in 1898, previously served as an icebreaker on the St. Lawrence River under the name *Tradewinds*, and before that as a Canadian coastguard cutter called *Gresham*. It was one of ten ships, including the famed *Exodus*, that were part of the clandestine operation known as Aliyah Bet, the attempted running of the British blockade during and especially after World War II.

Together with twenty-six other Americans on the *Hatikvah*, I set sail from Miami in February 1947. But the boat was in such disastrous shape that it had to make stops in Charleston and Baltimore for repairs before crossing the Atlantic and refueling in the Azores Islands off the coast of Portugal. From there it headed to Italy, where the passengers were waiting to secretly board.

Now it was on to Palestine – but our ship never made it. On May 17, 1947, a British destroyer pulled up alongside and demanded the ship's surrender as it neared the coast. It was towed into Haifa port, from where the passengers were sent to the internment camp in Cyprus – and these European Holocaust survivors who had survived concentration camps suddenly found themselves again behind barbed wire.

Eventually, everyone was taken to Haifa or Atlit and then allowed into Palestine little by little. By May 1948, almost seventy thousand men, women, and children had been brought to Palestine from ports in France, Italy, Yugoslavia, Greece, Bulgaria, and Romania.

Israel established Atlit as a national monument in 1987, restoring and reconstructing the historic camp with barbed wire fences, British watchtowers, and residential barracks.

Located around seven miles (12 km) south of Haifa, the Atlit Detention Camp Museum shares the names and stories of all 130,000 clandestine immigrants, activists, and volunteers detained at Atlit or in Cyprus. It serves as an educational center that teaches the history of *ha'apalah* (clandestine immigration) to the Land of Israel, helping visitors imagine the trauma of the survivors subjected to this imprisonment.

There is also an interactive exhibit that simulates the journey by sea and the storms, seasickness, failed engines, failed water tanks, paltry food supplies, poor sanitation, and hostile British blockade endured by the American boys who manned the so-called "rust bucket" vessels: the *Hatikvah*, the *Exodus*, the *Wedgewood*, the *Haganah*, the *Arlosoroff*, the *Ben Hecht*, the *Geula*, the *Jewish State*, the *Pan York*, and the *Pan Crescent*. The Airplane Experience exhibit tells of the clandestine immigration from Arab countries by air and land.

And me? I went back to the States after my adventure on the *Hatikvah* but was drawn back to the nascent Jewish state after a year. I joined the thirty-five hundred foreign volunteers called Mahal and became one of about five hundred who immigrated to help build the fledgling country.

Jonathan Kolber is Chairman and CEO of Anfield Ltd., his privately held investment firm.

Jonathan Kolber

The Zionist Dream in Yarkona and Ramot Hashavim

I was born in Montreal, Quebec, to a Jewish and Zionist family. My late father was a major real estate developer in North America, and my late mother was a Hebrew-speaking poet and script reader. After attending a Jewish parochial school in Montreal, I spoke decent Hebrew upon graduation. I then studied Near Eastern languages and civilizations at Harvard University, including a junior year abroad at the American University of Cairo.

I worked on Wall Street in the early eighties, returned to Montreal to work with the Bronfman family on investments, and set up a company called Claridge Israel with the incredible support of Charles Bronfman. By the 1990s, we were the biggest foreign family office investing in Israel in companies like Teva, Osem, and ECI Telecom. I ran Koor Industries as CEO for eight years and then became a partner in both the Viola group and the ION hedge funds.

Because of my Zionism and enormous financial commitment to the Israeli economy, I decided to make aliyah over thirty years ago.

In 1908, my late grandfather made aliyah to Palestine from a small village in Poland called Swislowicz, as part of the famous "Aliyah Shniyah" (Second Aliyah). He came with one sister, eventually was joined by three more sisters and a brother, and settled in the area of Kfar Malal, Ramot Hashavim, and Yarkona – three beautiful moshavim. Needless to say, the other six brothers and sisters who did not make aliyah were all murdered in the Holocaust, probably at Treblinka or maybe in the woods outside of Swislowicz.

My grandfather's name was Haim Maizel, and he served as a lieutenant in the Jewish Brigade of the Ottoman army in World War I after completing his officers' course in Constantinople. He served in Hebron and later in Gaza, where he was captured and sent to a British POW camp in Alexandria. He returned to Palestine, had trouble making a living, and traveled to Paris, where he studied electrical engineering at the Sorbonne. He then emigrated

From top left, clockwise:
One of the chicken coops, the 1930s (Photo: Joseph Photo)
Inauguration of Beit Ha'am Street in front of the Maizel family's land, 1951
Looking west toward Ramot Hashavim, 1930s. The area on the left, in front of the far group of houses (Hakerem Street), is the Maizel family's land.
A view of the silo of Ramot Hashavim, early 1940s. The house on the far right is probably the Maizel home. (Photo: Yoss Photography)

All photos courtesy of the Ramot Hashavim Archive Collection

I had achieved closure as part of the great circle of migration that my late grandfather started.

These two beautiful moshavim represented a Zionist dream fulfilled – lush green fields, chicken coops, and amazing citrus trees, and simple, clean homes and warm families with day jobs in the government, private sector, and professions.

Many years ago, I was let in on the family real estate drama. My late grandfather Haim actually owned (through a 999-year lease) twelve dunams in Ramot Hashavim that were acquired from the Israel Lands Authority in 1924 by his brother Shmuel. In 1969, Shmuel gave parts of the tract to several family members, with the hope that the family would eventually create a Maizel village. The sixty-dunam tract in the heart of this beautiful moshav is still owned by the descendants of the same families that moved here before the First World War.

My grandfather left his share to my late grandmother, who in turn left it to her daughters (my late mother and aunt). My aunt relinquished her share in an intra-family arrangement, and then my mother left hers to my late father, who bequeathed the land to our three children – Benjamin, Daniella, and Michael – and to my niece Olivia in Florida. The family had its divisions but is now unified in getting permission to zone and build on this great tract of land in what is now a very desirable location. We have reregistered the land many times in each generation with the land authorities in Israel (a nightmare!) and are doing so again.

Some members of the family want to build a Maizel family development, and others just want to sell their share. I don't know what our children will decide to do, but the wheels that started 113 years ago and continue to this day on the same tract of land represent to me my little slice of Zionism: love of the country and its fields, its fruit and produce, and return.

Haim Maizel (seated in the middle, bottom row), in the Jewish brigade of the Ottoman army, circa 1914

to New York City. Following a matchmaking effort with a girl from a nearby shtetl who lived in Montreal, he eventually married her and moved to Canada.

I first visited Israel when I was fifteen years old as part of a Zionist youth trip. I fell in love with the country, and every summer I found a reason to come back, pledging that I would eventually settle in Israel. Between different youth groups, summer work at the Jewish Agency, and other odd jobs, I always spent an enormous amount of time at Yarkona and Ramot Hashavim with my newly discovered Israeli cousins. They were enormously welcoming and loving, and when I finally made aliyah, I felt that

Sharon Harel-Cohen

Remembering Heroes at Exodus Memorial Garden

Sharon Harel-Cohen is Chairman of WestEnd Films. She has been involved in producing and financing over fifty films and has worked with numerous major film stars. Her father, Yossi Harel, commanded four ships for the Aiyah Bet illegal immigration movement to Mandatory Palestine in 1947.

Every day, in the early hours of the morning, I go for a walk along the Tel Aviv Promenade, followed by a swim in the sea. It has become a kind of happy ritual for me, which helped keep me sane through the COVID-19 pandemic.

I leave my home and walk through the romantic alleys of Neve Tzedek. From there, I turn north on the Tayelet (boardwalk) toward Gordon Beach. To my right, the hustle and bustle of the cityscape seems to be constantly changing, with new high-rise buildings springing up all the time. But my attention is on the Mediterranean Sea to my left. I look to the shore, taking in the same view that excited me as a child, which my parents loved so much. I take off my shoes and walk on the soft sand with the waves lapping at my feet. It is a precious moment for myself.

The sea is very meaningful to me and my family. My father, Yossi Harel, was a navy man. He was the commander of the *Exodus* and three other ships that brought refugees from Europe to Israel after the Second World War. He transported more than twenty-five thousand refugees in rusty old ships, struggling against the elements and the Royal Navy's blockade.

One of his ships, the *Exodus*, turned into the global symbol of the need for a Jewish state. The *Exodus* was a worn-out freight ship that was sold as scrap to the Haganah, an underground Jewish military organization of the pre-State days. Their plan was to transport Jewish men, women, and children – all displaced persons or survivors of the Holocaust – to Palestine. In 1947, *Exodus* left the docks of Sète, France, carrying 4,515 people. But when the ship reached Palestine's territorial waters, it was suddenly surrounded by British destroyers, and a bloody struggle ensued.

Attempting to make an example of it, the British towed the ship to Haifa and transferred the passengers onto three Royal Navy transports, which returned to France. The passengers refused to disembark, and the French authorities refused to forcibly remove the refugees. The British tried to wait them out, but the passengers, including many

Photo: Ori~

Photo: Snowman

orphaned children, forced the issue by declaring a hunger strike that lasted twenty-four days in the sweltering July heat.

By then, the plight of the ship's passengers had captured the world's attention. The whole world watched as the British forced the bedraggled passengers back to detention camps in Germany. It was too much for the world to take, and the huge public outcry helped gain a majority in the UN for the creation of the Jewish state.

The *Exodus* had such a powerful impact that Leon Uris wrote a best-selling novel about it in 1958 that was turned into a famous film, in which Paul Newman played my father.

I often think of the passengers catching the first glimpse of Israel's shores after all they had been through. They are commemorated in the Ha'apalah Memorial in London Garden, halfway along my walk, at the intersection with Bograshov Street. The memorial is made of six giant plates designed to look like a wave, with the prows of ships rising up as if landing on the beach. It commemorates all the ships that set out – those that made it and those that did not – recalling their names on the sculpted waves and illustrating their stories in photographs.

My father's funeral was held here. Navy ships fired salutes, and Shimon Peres and Ehud Barak eulogized him. Today the ships and their legends are the backdrop for a very lively scene. In this garden, you can always find children playing and adults drinking coffee; thousands of people come here every day for a walk or to enjoy the beautiful sunset. The whole place is teeming with life, exactly as my father would have liked.

Kira Radinsky

The Abandoned Boat at Dor Beach

For many long years, waves have eroded the sandstone rocks along Israel's northern coast, creating enchanting inlets at the site of the ancient Palestinian-Canaanite-Greek-Roman port city known as Dor, adopted as the modern name of this beach. The battered boat lies at the end of the beach, tucked behind endless shades of blue, heaps of shells on the sand, and reeds that shelter sea turtles. It is watched by thousands of shells, each one different from the next. One has thick strips, another narrow; one is dark, another pale; one is big, another small. Despite their differences, they share a similar fate – all were washed up onto this beach, with its dozens of tiny coves and cool breeze that spatters the salty water in our faces at sunset.

This fishing boat was born in the State of Israel in the 1960s. When it was only ten years old, it was shattered in a huge storm. When the captain sounded the distress signal, the SS *Panther* came to its rescue, trying with all its might to drag the fishing boat to safety. But its cable tore, and the fishing boat was swept ashore, where it became an inseparable part of the coastal landscape.

But small boats landed on this delightful beach even before the establishment of the State of Israel. After the horrors of the Second World War devastated the Jewish people in Europe, the struggle began to bring survivors to Palestine. The boats of the *ha'apalah* (the Aliyah Bet Jewish immigration to Palestine, illegal under the British Mandate) left the ports of Europe and evaded the British fleet in a desperate attempt to reach safe haven in Palestine. Some landed at Dor Beach. The local Jewish community organized to help the new arrivals. The Haganah (which formed the basis of the IDF after the establishment of the state) organized a military force with thousands of activists and volunteers. The Palyam (the Palmach sea naval force) sailed the *ha'apalah* ships, while kibbutz members and residents of coastal

Kira Radinsky is the CEO and CTO of Diagnostic Robotics, where the most advanced technologies in the field of artificial intelligence are harnessed to make healthcare better, cheaper, and more widely available. She previously served as eBay director of data science and IL chief scientist.

towns absorbed the new immigrants. Everyone worked together to save every individual. The *ha'apalah* movement became a major component in settling the land and helped lead to the establishment of the sovereign, independent State of Israel.

On December 25, 1945, the Aliyah Bet ship *Hannah Senesh* ran aground off the coast of Nahariya, and some 250 *ma'apilim*, together with the Italian crew of the ship, were rescued and brought ashore by the Palyam. As I stand on Dor Beach reflecting on the wreckage of a boat, I meditate on the poem "Response to an Italian Captain [after the Nighttime Disembarkation]," written by Natan Alterman, who was incredibly moved by the self-sacrifice of the non-Jewish ship captain who sailed the *Hannah Senesh*. In my view, this is the story of the State of Israel, in which each individual "bears his people upon his shoulders" – because this is how the state was built, one grain of sand on top of another..

Excerpt from "Response to an Italian Captain"

The wind lashed the sea,
and the sea lashed the ship;
You steered through the
tempest's commotion.
We drink to you Captain,
and lift the glass high;
We'll meet again on this ocean.

No Lloyds would insure your small,
secret craft,
Nor the perilous struggle it wages;
But though in the ship's log
no record be kept,
We'll chart it in history's pages.

This frail, hidden fleet,
grey and silent, will be
The subject of song and of story;
And many a captain, who hears
of the tale,
Will envy you, Captain, your glory.

The night hid the battle with wave
and with tide,
But our lads than the storm-wind
were stronger;
Oh, Captain, you saw how from ship
to the shore
Each swam with a refugee on his shoulder.
...
"The gates of the land are flung wide!
This was done by the lads who clambered aboard
And carried ashore their precious load."

– Natan Alterman, translated from the Hebrew by Marie Syrkin, *Blessed Is the Match* (Philadelphia: Jewish Publication Society, 1947)

Photo: Hagai Agmon-Snir (CC BY-SA 4.0)

Gideon Argov

The Night Sky in the Valley of the Cross

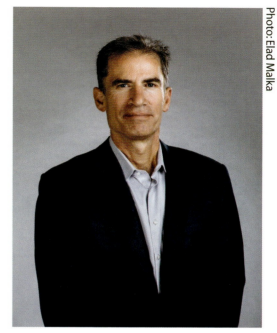

Gideon Argov is Managing Partner and Cofounder at New Era Capital Partners and an Advisory Director of Berkshire Partners in Boston. Gideon is a serial angel investor in Israeli technology companies. He holds a BA from Harvard University and an MBA from the Stanford Graduate School of Business.

The Jerusalem of my childhood was a small city on the crest of the Judean Hills, the ancient capital city of a relatively new democracy. There were three swimming pools in the city, one luxury hotel (the King David), and no Michelin-starred restaurants. We children were left largely on our own after school, free to hang out with our *chevre* (gang of friends) playing soccer and *stanga* (a kind of soccer played with small tennis balls on the street) and making evening "*kumzitz*" campfires in the fields across the road from our modest apartment blocks, where we would roast potatoes and sing songs that our parents taught us about the founding of Israel and the meaning of Zionism.

It was a beautiful and innocent childhood in a city with fewer than 200,000 inhabitants, divided by an armistice line into an Israeli and a Jordanian sector and – just as described in the 1967 song "Yerushalayim shel Zahav" by Naomi Shemer – "captivated by its own dreams."

Some of us had parents with numbers tattooed onto their forearms; they were mostly silent about what they endured, but their faces held a pinched sadness. All of us knew that Israel was a miracle and that its future was by no means certain.

Most residents of the city were secular or moderately observant; the ultra-Orthodox were a minority and largely concentrated in one or two neighborhoods. They were looked at as a vestige of the Diaspora – pale and frail, with none of the confidence and swagger that we as Israeli Sabras had. We didn't know any of them personally.

Our apartment was on the third floor of a 1960s concrete walk-up building, an ugly structure built to acccmmodate the rapid growth of the Jewish sector in the decades following independence. The apartment was small – a bedroom for my two sisters, a small one for me, and a convertible couch in the living room where my parents would sleep. In the winter, the whole apartment smelled of kerosene from the heating oil my parents would schlep up three flights of stairs in jerricans twice a week.

The pièce de résistance of the apartment was the balcony, which faced west and across open fields, across Azza Road and overlooking the neighborhoods of Givat Mordechai, Nayot, and Beit Hakerem. You could see for miles from our third-floor balcony. I loved nothing more than to sneak out of my bed under cover of darkness and stare at the nighttime scenery and lights.

Across from our neighborhood was an open area known as the Valley of the Cross, including an orchard, empty fields of flowers and rocks, and in its midst a large and imposing eleventh-century monastery built by Georgians during the reign of King Bagrat IV. We would take long walks in the valley on Saturdays, stopping to admire wildflowers or to find frogs, turtles, and even the occasional deer.

The night sky – particularly during the summer – was ablaze with billions of stars. The ambient man-made light pollution was minimal, and the Milky Way was clearly visible. Jerusalem was also relatively quiet at night, and in the valley, the sounds of jackals howling pierced the air. These images and sounds formed the basis for my enchantment with and love for the country where I was born.

During the Six-Day War of June 1967, Israel fought for its very existence against an array of larger armed forces. The Jordanian army had set up an artillery battery to the south of the city in the vicinity of the Arab village of Beit Zafafa. Israel in turn had stationed howitzers in the Valley of the Cross, aimed at the Jordanian positions several kilometers away. Our fathers had mostly been called up to reserve duty. As we spent the first nights of the war in ground-floor shelters, we witnessed firsthand the dueling artillery batteries firing at each other. The night sky was ablaze not with stars but with the red arcs of tracer bullets and the yellow explosions of artillery shells. We held our collective breath until – on the third day of combat – the scale and speed of Israel's victory became apparent.

Today Jerusalem has over a million residents, unified geographically but splintered into multiple and largely irreconcilable communities separated by faith, origin, economic status, and political affiliation. The Valley of the Cross continues to be an oasis of quiet and beauty in the midst of all this turmoil. I can only pray that the city and the country can find a safe path forward and that a hundred years from now, another generation of children will walk the trails of the Valley of the Cross, listen to the wails of the jackals at night, and look out at the twinkling stars.

Lili Ben-Ami

The Revolution Starts in Moshav Beit Zayit

Lili Ben-Ami is founder and CEO of the Michal Sela Forum for technological innovation in the prevention of femicide and domestic violence. She appeared on the 2021 Forbes World's 100 Most Powerful Women list and was awarded the 2021 Rapaport Prize and the Peres Center for Peace and Innovation Prize.

Moshav Beit Zayit is where I was born, built my home, and am raising my children. I serve as an elected official on the local council. My extended family lives on the moshav too: my parents, sisters and brother, uncles, and other relatives as well.

This is also where part of my soul was cut off, when my younger sister was cruelly murdered just a three-minute drive from my house. In October 2019, Michal Sela was only thirty-two years old when her husband murdered her in front of their baby daughter. An hour and a half earlier, she had driven me to my home after the two of us had attended an enjoyable women's workshop. In an exercise led by the workshop leader, Michal and I found ourselves staring into each other's eyes for two minutes. I recall her face and expression – strong, erect, beautiful. Several months later, I had to describe that night in court at the murder trial.

My mother's parents are Holocaust survivors, Hungarian-speakers who made aliyah from Yugoslavia and received a one-room apartment in the Baka neighborhood of Jerusalem in 1948. My grandfather was a partisan, and my late grandmother, Lili Kashticher (after whom I am named), survived Auschwitz-Birkenau. Fifty-two members of my grandmother's family were murdered in the Holocaust, including her brother and her father. I spent years researching the details of her story. I gave lectures about it and published articles. But it was only after Michal's murder that I understood for the first time what my grandmother had felt.

My father's parents made aliyah from Egypt, along with their extended family. In Egypt,

they lived a comfortable life in the city. The parents of my late grandmother, Allegra Shama Srur, owned three stores for groceries and textiles in Cairo. They lived in the Dahr neighborhood and maintained friendly relations with their Muslim neighbors, who attended the well-regarded Jewish school. When the State of Israel was founded, everything changed. Sanctions were imposed on Egypt's Jews. They were not allowed to work or to immigrate to Israel, and their property was stolen. In 1950, after living in a refugee camp in Italy and a tent camp in Pardes Hannah, then twenty-year-old Grandmother Allegra and her family were put on Jewish Agency buses. Along with other Egyptian and Yugoslavian families, they were taken to the Jerusalem Forest to build Moshav Beit Zayit.

Members of Kibbutz Nahalal came to Beit Zayit to teach the Arabic-speaking former city dwellers how to work the land, grow plums, and raise chickens. During the first decade, they had no electricity or other infrastructure. They lived in a one-room house with no bathroom, heated with kerosene, and bathed in a tub filled with water heated over their kerosene burner. Seventy years later, I built my dream house in the extended area of the moshav, near my parents' land. I was happy with my life, my work, and the family I had built with my husband Eran. I was living my dream – until it was shattered by the thrust of a knife.

Photo: Hagai Agmon-Snir (CC BY-SA 4.0)

After my sister was murdered, I felt overwhelmed with questions. Could Michal have been saved? I researched the topic of femicide and domestic violence, and I found answers. Yes, Michal could have been saved. But in Israel, this field has remained static ever since the state was founded. The state only acts after physical violence. Michal, like half of femicide victims, didn't suffer from physical violence prior to the murder. So in reality, as of the time of her murder, there was no prevention.

This is why I founded the Michal Sela Forum, a nonprofit organization that aims to prevent domestic violence and femicide through technology and innovation. Using out-of-the-box thinking and engaging new players, we are developing creative, interdisciplinary solutions. We promote dozens of start-ups and partner with technology giants such as Google, Meta, and Microsoft, as well as government ministries and the president of Israel.

Grandmother Allegra and Grandmother Lili came here at the founding of the state, from East and West. They suffered only because of the time and place in which they were born. Femicide is not a circumstance of fate. Together we will build an Iron Dome against domestic violence. When Michal Sela's baby daughter grows up, she will take her own daughter to visit her mother's grave in Moshav Beit Zayit. She will tell her that once upon a time in the State of Israel, there was such a thing as femicide. But today, we live in a new reality in which women are safe in their homes. Zero murders per year. May her memory be a revolution..

Achiya Klein

Kibbutz Kfar Etzion: Full of Life

I was born on Kibbutz Kfar Etzion, where we grew up with an awareness of the special heritage of this place. We learned about the people imbued with faith and Zionism who came to Kfar Etzion in 1943. This was the third attempt at settling this site. Eventually they were joined by Holocaust survivors. Four settlements were established in Gush Etzion: Kfar Etzion, Ein Zurim, Masu'ot Yitzchak, and Revadim. The settlers labored hard to hold on to the land. They worked the rocky earth and faced water shortages and snowy weather. They built a sanatorium where people came in the summer to enjoy clear mountain air. The kibbutz members moved out of their homes into tents, and the vacationers stayed in the members' homes.

Second Lieutenant Achiya Klein *was blinded by a Hamas bomb attack in 2013 as he took part in an IDF operation to uncover a terror tunnel leading from Gaza into Israel. Today he is a Paralympic rowing athlete and represents various nonprofit organizations for disabled IDF veterans.*

Photo: Eitan Ya'aran

Photo: Deror avi (CC BY-SA 3.0)

Photo: Refa'el Yaniger

In 1947–1948, the locals fought bravely in grueling battles. Throughout that period, the kibbutz continued to grow and maintain its cultural life. Due to the difficult security situation, the women and children were sent in a convoy to the Ratisbonne Monastery in Jerusalem. Families were separated, and the tension was extreme. On 3 Iyar 5708 (May 12, 1948), the decisive battle in the region began, and on 4 Iyar (May 13), "the Queen [code name for Gush Etzion] has fallen" – Gush Etzion succumbed to the enemy, and 240 Jewish fighters were killed. Members of the other settlements were taken prisoner by the Jordanians.

David Ben-Gurion, Israel's first prime minister, said when he declared the establishment of the state: "The State of Israel is established by the light of the burning torch of Gush Etzion."

Many children were orphaned, and mothers became widows. They lived together for a time in the Givat Aliyah neighborhood of Tel Aviv. The children continued to meet, and in their games, they recalled the landscapes of their childhood on the kibbutz.

Gush Etzion was liberated during the Six-Day War. By that time, the children born here before the establishment of the state had become soldiers. The desire to return home was powerful.

To me, the story of the fall and revival of Gush Etzion represents the significance of the Jewish people. Physical destruction and ruin did not break the will to build. The children returned to the hill from which they had been banished nineteen years earlier, and they established Kibbutz Kfar Etzion. From its inception, the return home was intertwined with the desire to transmit the site's heritage. A field school was established to tell the history of Gush Etzion and the Hebron hills – the same places where our ancestors walked. Abraham walked here with his son Isaac on their way to the binding on Mount Moriah.

Etzion Synagogue (Photo: Deror avi [CC BY-SA 3.0])

Later, guesthouses were built, and today, tourists of all ages come to enjoy the unique views, the history, and the clean air. Family groups have Shabbat and festive gatherings here. Gush Etzion also has several springs for hiking, bike paths, and the longest zipline in Israel.

The new multimedia presentation at the Gush Etzion Heritage Center introduces the story of the establishment of Gush Etzion, past and present. It illustrates the unique history of this place in an experiential, exciting manner. The presentation is an area designated for commemorating Gush Etzion's fallen in the War of Independence. The children who returned to rebuild the home that was destroyed chose living remembrance – a memorial that transmits the heritage of a place that will be full of life.

The presentation is screened using innovative technology and is available in three languages. Its tone is majestic, as the fall was deeply painful – but we did not stop there. The site was rebuilt, and today it flourishes. A letter written by a Kfar Etzion member to his family states, "If we are not privileged to see it, our children will be." Indeed, today many communities are growing in Gush Etzion, with many types of educational institutions, factories, mountain agriculture (orchards, vineyards, flower nurseries), specialty wineries, shopping centers, and restaurants – the place is blossoming and full of life.

Nadav Zafrir

Roots at the Military Cemetery in Kibbutz Kiryat Anavim

Nadav Zafrir *is Cofounder of Team8 and Managing Partner of Team8 Group. He previously served as Commander of Unit 8200, Israel's elite military intelligence unit.*

In a narrow valley down the slopes of the Judean Hills lies an exceptional piece of Zionist history. I am very fortunate that this place is also my childhood landscape. Growing up, I was in awe of the stories and legacies left behind by generations before me. If there is holiness in a person's life, this location is as close as it gets for me.

The green and peaceful surroundings of the cemetery are a sharp contrast to the dramatic stories buried in its ground. The Kiryat Anavim military cemetery is the resting place of some of Israel's legendary pioneers, innovators, and combatants. It is the only cemetery in the country dedicated to the fallen soldiers from one specific brigade, the Palmach Harel Brigade. Alongside the adjacent Kibbutz Kiryat Anavim – where I grew up – it reveals a unique angle on Zionist history and is in my opinion a good representation of the miracle of Israel.

If you choose the rugged arrival option, you can follow the trail from Radar Hill to the top of the cemetery, where you will come upon the Deer Monument, designed by the sculptor Menahem Shemi, father of Jimmy, one of the fallen soldiers.

The monument is made of polished limestone carved from the nearby Castel quarry. The walls inside are covered with plaques featuring photos and the names of the fallen. Each picture tells a story of men and women who were a model of *safra v'saifa* (Hebrew סִפְרָא וְסַיְפָא, "the book and the sword").

In January 1948, two months into the War of Independence, all units in the Jerusalem corridor and hills were grouped as the Harel Brigade, under Yitzhak Rabin's command. Their mission: to keep the road to Jerusalem open and free the city from the Arab siege.

The Kiryat Anavim military cemetery

Photo: YoavR (CC BY-SA 3.0)

In *Yona Ve-Na'ar* (*A Pigeon and a Boy*), Israeli author Meir Shalev tells the story of those days in his mesmerizing style, recalling how the clanging of picks digging fresh graves in the limestone rang in the ears of the soldiers as they went out to battle.

Carved on these graves are the names of the fallen. You will notice their particularly young age. Some are memorialized by their nicknames only, as they were Holocaust survivors who had just gotten off the boats from war-ravaged Europe, and their names were yet unknown. This cemetery is also the resting place of some of Israel's most legendary warriors.

Kibbutz Kiryat Anavim, home to the Harel Brigade, is a fascinating piece of history on its own. It is the first kibbutz in the area and the fifth in Israel. Its original founders arrived from Ukraine. My grandparents joined them in 1936 with the Gordonia group from Galicia, Poland.

In those early pioneering days, farming in the rocky terrain was near impossible. Kibbutz members moved rocks with nothing but their bare hands to clear land for agriculture. Water was scarce, and the land was dry. But with time, they were able to lay water pipes and plant grapes, peaches, plums, and cherries.

They were people who came from a corrupt and war-ridden Europe with a utopian vision to create a new moral society. They knew nothing of farming but turned barren lands into blossoming fields. They had no combat experience but bravely defended their land.

My father ran the dairy farm on the kibbutz. I grew up with stories of importing cows from Holland and using trial and error with special feeding methods to get the first cows to yield over ten thousand liters a year, which is a lot, even by today's standards.

My father was also one of the first to experiment with artificial insemination. My mother likes to tell how on the day that I was born, my father came in with the news that a difficult calving was underway. And so she set off to the hospital and he to the cowshed. The calf that was born on that day grew up to become a sire by the name of Ararat who for years was one of the few breeding bulls of the nation.

Today, I visit the Kiryat Anavim military cemetery at least once a year on Yom Hazikaron (Israel's Memorial Day) to honor the fallen Harel Brigade soldiers and to visit the graves of my father, grandparents, and my uncle Nadav, who fell while serving in the tank infantry and after whom I was named. To the officers and delegations I sometimes bring here, I say that this place is a time capsule of Israel. Look inside, and you will see the origins of Israeli innovation, entrepreneurship, defense, community, agriculture, and society. The cemetery tells the remarkable story of people who overnight became farmers, warriors, innovators, community makers, and state founders. The contrast between the memorial tombs and the voices of children playing in the kibbutz – representing life and growth – is a part of the place's magic.

Take a leisurely stroll around the cemetery. Feel, observe, and embrace the deep roots of nation building planted in the ground. To me, this is a rare and inspiring piece of history. And if you ever wish to understand the wonder that is the State of Israel, be sure to visit here.

Pierre Besnainou is a businessman and a former Jewish community leader in France. From 2005 to 2007, he was President of the European Jewish Congress. He is a member of the board of governors at the Peres Center for Peace and Innovation.

Pierre Besnainou

The Olive Trees at Kibbutz Revivim

I spent my youth in a Mediterranean country of harmonious landscapes. It was there, in Tunisia, surrounded by the soothing aura of the everlasting blue sea, that I grew into adulthood. At age seventeen, I left for France, carrying with me the memory of olive trees extending as far as the eye could see. Years later, I would see them again in another land tinged by the blue sea. A Promised Land, rough and dry, where everything had to be built. A land that inspired imagination, a land that required settlement, tending, nourishment, growth, and production. A place that allowed invention and needed protection.

My Israel is and always will be the Israel of kibbutzim. Where David Ben-Gurion inspired, with his vision of a rich land. Where those pioneers worked the land, transforming the rugged terrain into flourishing green fields with their own hands.

My Israel is the special pink light of the sun rising and setting over the sands of the Negev. Where the alleyways connect rather than separate the houses and those who live in them. Where nothing really belongs to anyone, but everything belongs to everyone. The kibbutzim, where men and women work together and where harshness and sweetness coexist, making these privileged and protected places unique in the world. I admire the creative vision of those who established these kibbutzim, where the focus is community, and where individuals stand aside for the greater good of humanity.

My Israel is Kibbutz Revivim, symbol of the difficult birth of the country. The promise and enthusiasm of an untilled land with its unknowns and challenges. Exhilarating. Constructed by the British, Revivim has developed a wonderful ecosystem, cultivating greenery and olive trees from the harsh, sandy conditions of the desert. Its members have fought thirst, isolation, and Egyptian forces. The people of Revivim have managed to hide, to

resist, and to adapt. Following agricultural farming, Kibbutz Revivim chose to undertake dairy farming with modern techniques, as well as integrating sophisticated irrigation systems for their olive trees. Faced with industrial demands for efficiency, speed, and sophistication, Revivim has adapted skillfully while preserving its values and maintaining its raison d'être.

Revivim is my Israel. In the footsteps of those men I have admired – of Shimon Peres, who guided me through the kibbutz with his friendship – I contemplate this land. I walk on this cultivated soil, bathing in the pink sunlight, admiring what its members have accomplished. I walk along these paths, in the shade of the foliage. These olive trees create a link between my childhood and my present. I remember that we are – here and there – children of the Mediterranean.

Ayelet Nahmias-Verbin

The Circle of Moshav Nahalal

Ayelet Nahmias-Verbin, wife of Ivri and mother of three, is a lawyer and former member of Knesset on behalf of the Zionist Union. She is Chairperson of the Israel Export Institute, a board member in leading companies in Israel, and also heads the Jewish Agency's Fund for Victims of Terror and JReady.

Once a year, as we drive toward Moshav Nahalal, instead of turning right to the moshav, we continue driving past the junction and turn left, into Nahalal Cemetery at the nearby archaeological site Tel Shimron. The headstones there recount an impressive span of Israel's history since the First Aliyah, around the turn of the twentieth century.

Each year, we wander around the cemetery with our children, searching for the headstones of my great-grandfather and great-grandmother, Michael and Nechamah Karasik, who were among the seven first residents of Nahalal. Even though I never had the privilege of living there, our children know that they are fifth-generation descendants of the founders of Nahalal, which is first mentioned in the Book of Joshua.

Tel Shimron looks out over the beautiful Jezreel Valley, and it is the resting place of Moshe Dayan (and his two wives and children) and Musa Peled. This is also where the late Rona Ramon requested to have her husband Ilan and her son Assaf laid to rest. Rona's memorial stone watches over them both, as if to ensure nothing will disturb their rest. Also buried here are my great-uncle Yakovik, killed in the Sinai War, and my great-uncle Amnon (Nonik), whose son Alon is the latest to continue our farm.

I say "our" even though I never lived in Nahalal, because my Israel is there.

Nahalal is the only town in the world that is planned in a circle, following the design of architect Richard Kauffman. The design is intended to symbolize the settlers' aspiration to equality.

Nahalal is where I learned how to stroke newborn lambs, where I could touch the soil even though we'd become city people, and where I learned how to drive a tractor before the legal age. This is where my heart skips a beat when we pass the big silo, the corner store, and the grass commons next to the cultural hall.

History took a turn thanks to my grandmother, Sarah Stern (nee Kresik), who transformed us into residents of Tel Aviv. Sarah, the Kresiks' eldest daughter, left Nahalal at seventeen to serve in the British Army's Auxiliary Territorial Service together with Sonia Peres (wife of former president Shimon Peres). While serving in Egypt, she met Avraham Stern of Zefat, and they were married in 1945, on the Nahalal commons.

Avraham served in the British train brigade for another year, and when he returned, they decided to try their luck in Tel Aviv. There they established Tamar Cafe. Through it, Sarah, the quintessential moshav woman and skilled horseback rider, became a founding member of the cultural scene in the first Hebrew city, and the cafe served as a magnet for journalists, artists, and politicians.

On August 16, 2021 (8 Elul 5751), Nahalal celebrated the hundredth anniversary of its founding. Although I didn't grow up there, I am inexorably drawn to it. I understood from a young age that something special had happened there, that it wasn't just another random place, but rather a kernel of Zionism and of strengthening Jewish settlement.

Undoubtedly, the most famous person to have come from Nahalal was the heroic and colorful Moshe Dayan. Few members of the Dayan family remain there, but their family is inextricably connected to Nahalal.

Likewise for my family. Every Friday, my grandmother would close the Tamar Cafe on the corner of Shenkin and Ahad Ha'am Streets in Tel Aviv. She would load the car with goodies, and off we would go to visit our family on the moshav. We would race up the path toward the chicken coops and dairy barns. The best Saturdays were when we helped out in the fields, picking flowers, eggplants, or watermelons.

To this day, many Nahalal residents take on important roles in the IDF and in Israel's politics and economy. Students of the Nahalal Agricultural School also became important public figures, such as my grandmother's beloved counselor Hannah Senesh. The Israeli writer Meir Shalev, grandson of founding member Aharon Ben Barak, wrote novels set in the picturesque scenery of Nahalal.

Nahalal is my Israel because it influenced my worldview – my belief in agriculture and industry as the cornerstones of Israel's economy, in entrepreneurship and initiative.

In her old age, Grandma Sarah spent many weekends with us. When Shabbat was over, sometimes she wasn't sure whether she was in Tel Aviv or in Nahalal. The big city was in her heart, but Nahalal was in her soul. The circle of Nahalal was never perfect, but it is a perfect whole.

Jossef Avi Yair "Jucha" Engel

The Legacy of Mitzpe Yair, Kibbutz Ramat Rachel

Mitzpe Yair (Yair Overlook) is an observation point located on Kibbutz Ramat Rachel near Jerusalem, at the edge of a fascinating archeological site and atop fortifications from the War of Independence. The lookout was built in 1999 in memory of Yair Engel, a third-generation kibbutz member whose grandparents were among its founders. On the eve of Chanukah in 1996, Engel and fellow soldier Matan Polivoda were killed in a diving accident while serving in the Shayetet 13 marine commando unit (Israel's Navy Seals).

The lookout is situated in the Lurie Garden, a pine forest planted in 1937 in memory of Joseph Lurie. At 2,690 feet (820 m) above sea level, the lookout is one of the highest points around Jerusalem.

We chose this location for the observation point for three reasons.

The first is the site's historical significance. The lookout is constructed near a guard tower that dates to the First and Second Temple eras, through the Roman and Byzantine conquests and up to the Muslim period. It controlled an intersection of strategic importance, both then and now. The junction's north-south axis was originally known as "Ancestors' Road" or "King's Road" – today's Highway 60. The west-east axis runs from the coastal plain through the Valley of Rephaim in the German Colony of Jerusalem, to the Dead Sea. From biblical days until the Six-Day War, dominating this crossroads meant control over the southern entrance to Jerusalem. Thus, the lookout links ancient Jewish history to the modern State of Israel, which Yair served faithfully.

Jossef Avi Yair "Jucha" Engel *is kibbutz secretary and son of the founders of Kibbutz Ramat Rachel. His son Yair of blessed memory was a third-generation member.*

Photos: Jossef Avi Yair "Jucha" Engel

The second reason is that the site is 2.8 miles (4.5 km) from Bethlehem, birthplace of both King David and Jesus, and 2.8 miles (4.5 km) from their burial sites in Jerusalem, at the center of a 5.6-mile (9 km) axis that represents the cradle of Western civilization for the past two thousand years.

The third reason is that the observation point offers a spectacular view of Jerusalem. From it, we can see (from north to south) the Temple Mount; the new city center; the Bridge of Strings; the Knesset and government buildings; the Israel Museum; Katamon and San Simon neighborhoods; Shaare Zedek Medical Center and behind it, Mount Herzl and the IDF cemetery; Bayit VeGan neighborhood; Malcha shopping mall, Pais Arena Jerusalem and Teddy Stadium; the Science Center; the Givat Massua, Ora, Aminadav, Emek Refaim, and Gilo neighborhoods; Mount Gilo, Beit Jala neighborhood, Neve Daniel, and further south toward Gush Etzion.

Mitzpe Yair was planned and constructed by artist Ran Morin, whose grandparents were among the founders of the kibbutz. Ran has designed many other sculptures in Israel, including the *Olive Tree Columns* environmental sculpture on the east edge of the kibbutz and a hanging sculpture in Old Jaffa.

The observation point is constructed mostly of local flint rock. Eighty dressed stones adorn its sides, and in the center, the artist transplanted an oak tree from the kibbutz. A spiral stairway connects the upper portion of the walkway with the base. The spiral concept was taken from the proto-Aeolic carvings found in the archeological dig nearby. On the upper level, the history of the site is carved into the rock, along with a map of the landscape.

The shelter at the observation point is covered with grapes of the Mitzpe variety, developed by Israel's Agricultural Research Organization – Volcani Center. Beside it, we planted a grove of trees native to Israel. One of the trees is an etrog,

like the ones brought to the nearby fortress by the Persians some twenty-five hundred years ago.

At the entrance to the observation point is a memorial stone chiseled in the shape of a basketball. As a boy, Yair dreamed of becoming a professional basketball player, and he was a member of Hapo'el Jerusalem youth basketball team. But after a transformational 1994 youth trip to Holocaust sites in Poland, his new goal was to participate in an elite combat unit of the IDF.

After Yair's death, a notebook of his poems was found in his room; one was "Six Million Brothers," which he wrote during the trip to Poland. Songwriter Moshe Yosef set the poem to music, and David Daor made its debut performance in 2016 at the closing ceremony of the March of the Living, while standing atop the ruins of the crematoria at Birkenau. This was where Yair had stood to read the poem at the closing ceremony of his trip in 1994 – the same place where in 1943, his grandfather Shraga had been selected for forced labor to remove the corpses of victims from the crematoria.

Lieutenant General Gadi Eizenkot

In the Footsteps of Warriors – Amir Trail

I was born in Poriya Hospital in Tiberias, but my Israel extends the entire length and breadth of the state, from Dan in the north all the way down to Eilat, where I grew up. Our homeland is replete with sites commemorating our national and historical heritage. The site I chose to highlight is Amir Trail in Adamit Park, which honors the memory of Lieutenant Colonel Amir Meital, who fell in a battle against terrorists in Lebanon on 1 Tevet 5749 (December 9, 1988).

For the generation of soldiers and commanders who served in the 1970s, Lebanon became the front for operational activity and major combat. Amir Meital was one of the many commanders and fighters who served the IDF's goal of protecting the settlements in the north. Amir grew up in Hadera; at fourteen, he decided to attend a military boarding school. He was drafted into the Golani Brigade and served as commander of Battalion 12, until he fell while leading a foray deep inside Lebanon. After Amir was buried in Hadera, his family and comrades initiated a memorial project in the area from which he had launched the attack. Amir Trail is a walking route that begins in the main parking lot of Adamit Park and winds above Nachal Betzet, the northernmost of Israel's rivers that flow into the Mediterranean Sea. The trail passes through a nature preserve and lovely orchards with a lookout point offering a panoramic view of Haifa Bay, the Mediterranean, and the Western Galilee.

Each year on the holiday of Simchat Torah – the birthday of this brave, patriotic fighter – his family and friends meet and walk along the marked trail to the Keshet Cave. The path takes them through an enchanting area of hilly terrain, Galilee shrubbery, and orchards.

Lieutenant General Gadi Eizenkot was the twenty-first Chief of General Staff of the Israel Defense Forces (2015–2019).

At the exit point, hikers enjoy a view of both Israel and Lebanon. The journey combines past, present, and future, at the flashpoint of a highly sensitive border. Here we can see the potential for development and prosperity on both sides, for the well-being of the residents of both countries.

Miriam Peretz

A Sense of Mission at Nabi Samuel: Samuel's Tomb

Miriam Peretz is an Israeli educator and public speaker. After two of her sons fell in battle during their service in the Israel Defense Forces, Peretz became a lecturer on Zionism and living with loss. She was the recipient of the Israel Prize for lifetime achievement in 2018.

Nabi Samuel or Samuel's Tomb offers one of the most beautiful panoramic views of Jerusalem. Its history spans many periods. Jewish tradition identifies this site as the burial place of the prophet Samuel, the only son of Hannah. She swore that if she gave birth to a son, she would dedicate him to God. Today it is a pilgrimage site for Jews, Christians, and Muslims. It can be identified by the Crusader fortress that stands at the top of the hill.

The story of Samuel is that of a mother's longing for a son. In the biblical story, Elkanah had two wives, Penina and Hannah. "Penina had children, but Hannah had no children" (I Samuel 1:2). Hannah was barren and bitter, full of sorrow and pain. But she refused to submit to these circumstances, and she acted with quiet and modest determination. Her prayer is the plea of a barren woman who refuses to give up and believes that God will answer her request. Her silent prayer is simple, yet she weeps copiously while expressing her distress.

When God finally answers her prayer, and her son Samuel is born, "because I have asked him of the Lord" (I Samuel 1:20), she emphasizes, "For this child I prayed" (I Samuel 1:27). Her emotional prayer of thanks teaches us that we must not despair of God's mercy. When Samuel grows older, she takes him to Eli the priest at the tabernacle in Shiloh and consecrates him to serve God.

I find it deeply symbolic that in this very place, at Nabi Samuel, many Jewish soldiers were killed. The Harel Brigade fought here during the War of Independence and that same brigade reconquered the site in the Six-Day War.

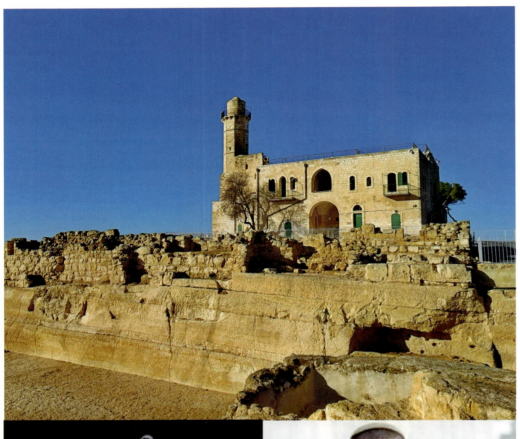

Above: *Major Eliraz Peretz*

Left: *First Lieutenant Uriel Peretz*

The soldiers of the IDF, heroes of the Jewish people, were also born out of deep longing and anticipation, as were my two sons, First Lieutenant Uriel Peretz and Major Eliraz Peretz, who fell in defense of our homeland. Every Jewish mother says, "For this child I prayed." We prayed to see them live and build families, but they gave their lives for the rebirth of the State of Israel. They dreamed and fell in defense of the state. Many who died were only children, yet they felt a deep sense of obligation and mission to serve their homeland.

Every generation has its own special mission. Samuel the Prophet had a mission, as well. He ushered in a new era by stabilizing the regime, and eventually he crowned King David, who founded Jerusalem. For this reason, this site is an important symbol of the rebirth of Jerusalem.

According to tradition, Samuel died on 28 Iyar – today celebrated as Jerusalem Day, commemorating the reunification of Jerusalem. Jerusalem is the nexus of the dreams and longing of every Jew. This is why I decided to locate the memorial for my sons at the foot of Samuel's Tomb. The Brothers' Promenade commemorating Uriel and Eliraz Peretz is on Road 436 and commands a view of all of Jerusalem. This is the Jerusalem that I dreamed of when I was a child in Morocco. I had the privilege of fulfilling the dream of immigrating to Eretz Yisrael, building a home, and raising my children here. Following the peace agreement with Egypt, I had to leave my home in Ofira at Sharm al-Sheikh, and I went to live in Givon and Givat Ze'ev, very near Jerusalem.

Every Shabbat, I used to walk to Nabi Samuel with my sons Uriel and Eliraz. The Brothers' Promenade overlooks Jerusalem, because we can only go up to Jerusalem and rebuild it when we are united in love, like the brotherly love that my sons shared. "In their lives, even in their death they were not divided" (II Samuel 1:23).

In addition, the choice of this site is connected to Eliraz's last meeting with his wife Shlomit, two weeks before he was killed. He chose to meet her at the Western Wall. Tears filled his eyes as he pointed toward Jerusalem and said, "See – we're fighting for this city, and if I must give my life for it, I will." Two weeks later, he fell in battle in the Gaza Strip.

From this promenade, we see Jerusalem – so many dreamed of it, so many died for it.

PART II

NATURE
The Land of Milk and Honey

Photo: Amichay Zini

Dan Ariely

The Brilliant Scars of Makhtesh Ramon

There are many types of scenery in Israel. In fact, it is hard to imagine more variety anywhere in the world in such close proximity. There are mountains and hills, forests and trees, the sea and beaches, and then, of course, the desert. For me, looking at the desert – but more importantly, walking in it – is the deepest and most intimate experience. In the desert, I feel as if I'm seeing the earth naked below me, stretched to the horizon and marked with the scars of time, sun, and the harshest conditions. In other parts of our day-to-day life, the earth is just there, not very visible and mostly hidden by roads, trees, and houses. In the desert, I feel that I see the earth as it is and as it has been for ages.

But it's not just that I love the desert – there are parts of it I especially gravitate to. My unsupported theory for what makes some parts of nature even more breathtaking is that they include a deep aspect of change.

If we were to make a list of all the places where we stand in awe of beauty, many of them, I think, would be places where we see a change. Beaches, cliffs, sunsets: the sand becomes the waves, flat land becomes a mountain, day becomes night. In the Negev Desert, there is one place where we can see a particularly striking change, and that is the Ramon Crater, Makhtesh Ramon. This crater, for me, is an emotional magnet. When I travel anywhere in the south of Israel, whatever my destination may be, I always seem to find myself at this crater at some point. Don't get me wrong, I love many things about the desert, but the crater holds some special magical power over me.

Makhtesh Ramon wasn't formed by a dramatic event like a meteor crashing into the earth or a major volcanic eruption (though a volcano did erupt there only a few thousand years ago). Rather, it was formed slowly over time. Millions of years ago, it was covered by the ocean, but slowly the ocean receded, valleys and hills were formed inside the crater, mountains were created around it, fossils were left behind, and rock in a range from red to yellow to creamy pink was created. All of these brilliant scars were left over time.

Dan Ariely is the James B. Duke Professor of Psychology & Behavioral Economics at Duke University and a founding member of the Center for Advanced Hindsight. He is a three-time New York Times bestselling author.

When I'm in the desert, I feel connected to the earth in a unique way. It's a basic and primitive feeling connecting me to the rocks, hills, canyons, and marks of history. In general, one of my personal flaws is that I find it very difficult to sit still for any amount of time and just observe things around me. But when I stop at the edge of Makhtesh Ramon and look around at the extraordinary beauty, the rest of the world disappears, and I feel connected, present, and calm. Maybe this is why I keep coming back.

Indeed, I'm here now, as I write these words, on a prolonged coffee break with Ron and Moran, my two best friends. We're hiking Gishron Canyon, which marks the end of the Israel National Trail in the south near Eilat.

And now, it is time to stop writing and turn to look and focus on the desert around me.

Stav Shaffir

Finding Clarity at Hod Akev

Stav Shaffir *is the youngest woman ever elected to the Knesset, where she served for eight years and was Chair of the Transparency Committee. A social entrepreneur and founder of the Shira Center for young adults with special needs, she previously led the 2011 Israeli social justice protests.*

I was a young woman of seventeen, with a big pack on my back and a topographical map in my hand, bathed in moonlight and the spirit of adventure. Panting with exertion, I reached Hod Akev, my favorite peak, 1,890 feet (576 meters) above sea level. The sun peeped out from behind pink clouds, beyond the Negev Mountains. This site offers the most beautiful view of Ramat Boker and the Zin Valley, of Ein Avdat and the remains of the ancient Negev commercial center, built in the center of the Spice Route between Petra and Gaza. In ancient times, this was one of the most important trade routes, used to transport luxury products such as silk, spices, and perfumes to Europe, connecting the Middle East over thousands of miles. Today, the Israel National Trail passes nearby.

Before me lies a modern enclave – not of desert merchants, but of students and researchers. This was the home and burial place of David Ben-Gurion, Israel's first prime minister. The story is told that one day, Ben-Gurion passed by this place on his way back from a military exercise. Seeing a cabin and a group of tents, he stopped his vehicle and discovered a group of young pioneers without political affiliation, who had fought for this place during the War of Independence. After the war, they felt that the only way they could truly protect it was to go live there. Ben-Gurion was so impressed that later he sent them a letter. He wrote that he'd never envied anyone before, but during his visit there, he was unable to suppress that very feeling. "Why have I not been able to participate in such a pioneering act?" When he took a break from politics, he went to live in a tiny cabin, here on Sde Boker.

Everyone, even Ben-Gurion, harbors an inner longing to fulfill a vision not yet achieved. Throughout my childhood, I dreamed of being a member of Ben-Gurion's generation, the generation of Israel's founders, the pioneers and fighters. They were the ones who dreamed of a State of Israel when it was still an implausible fantasy, throughout the horrors of the Holocaust in Europe and violence against Jews in the Middle East. Yet they did more than dream – they made sacrifices to realize that dream. To me, the ability to take a seemingly impossible dream and transform it into reality is the very essence of the Israeli character. If only we could take all our current dreams and realize that we have the power to make them happen – peace with our neighbors, a free Middle East, a state where all citizens enjoy the opportunity to live respectably – our future would change. We have the necessary creativity and willingness to work hard. But it is the mission of our generation to relearn the belief that this is possible.

As a teenager, whenever I wanted to dream big, I would always go down to the Negev. Sometimes I took a sleeping bag and spent the night out in the desert. The spot I loved the most was Sde Boker. Unlike in the crowded city, I felt so small out in the enormous desert – I was just another grain of sand. I felt that I could surrender completely. I could trust. It was a sense of freedom that I never felt anywhere else.

When I went into politics and became too busy to go wandering around in nature, I would snatch tiny moments of quiet in the desert – between a town hall meeting in the Arava and a work tour in Mitzpe Ramon. I used to stop my car on the side of the road and announce to my team that now we would sit and look at Hod Akev, even if only for a few minutes. In our crowded country, it was a vital break from the noise outside, which can be confusing. It was an opportunity to go on a short journey through the deliberations and dilemmas of the day and solve them so as to return to Jerusalem and implement them.

The Children of Israel spent decades wandering the desert, and perhaps something of that has remained with us. To find our destination, to reach our utopia – whether that means the land of milk and honey or the solution to a major problem – we all need a little bit of desert. Only after we've moved outside our comfort zone and gotten a little lost will we find the answer at the end of the path.

Photos: Mboesch (CC BY-SA 4.0)

Tal Ohana

Belonging in the Desert: Yeruham

Tal Ohana is the mayor of Yeruham, the first woman to serve in the position. She is the fourth generation of immigrants from Morocco, who came to Yeruham in its early years. Tal holds a master's degree from the Lauder School of Government, Diplomacy and Strategy at IDC Herzliya.

For years I've been traveling to it and inside it,
full of longing for something I haven't been able to know.
My greatest prayers are carried
through its infinite spaces.
They still honor
the remnants that we left behind.
The story of our wandering begins thousands of years ago
in the beautiful Sahara Desert,
where I return each fall in an endless search,
to pause in my steps and return to myself, without the dust of the road.
This story continues on to the noble Negev Desert,
this place of creation and simplicity, of wind, intimacy, and depth.
In its nonexistent mercy, it grants us
meaning
in life.

That's why the Torah was given in the desert.

To be born in the desert
is to know you always have a place
to create
something out of nothing,
something out of fire.

To know that you have air
in those moments when you've reached the peaks
and those times when you lose hope.
All you have to do is dream
and remember that you'll always have land
to return to.

It will always be there,
constant and present,
and it will teach you
the secret of renewal.

In years when there is no one to water its clods
and in years when it overflows its banks,
it will blossom.

We, the people of the desert –
the landscape of our homeland –
we have strength
and simplicity.
A constant prayer for rain from the heavens,
joy distilled from sunsets and sunrises,
and stories of our heritage, of our pioneering
grandmother and grandfather, four generations ago.
They created a life
of simplicity and grace
between hills and valleys
of pride
in fulfilling the vision of the founders of the Jewish
state
in the Land of Israel.

The future of the desert
is in technology
and tradition
that will preserve the gifts of nature,
the spirit of humanity
and its right to fulfill.

As the leader of a desert community
between crater and lake,
I feel that I belong
and I always remember
to plant the heavens.

Tchia Efron Klinger, a former Tel Aviv lawyer, was born in Israel in 1958, has been sharing a life with David for over forty-five years, is the mother of five sons and a profound believer in love and justice.

Tchia Efron Klinger

Big Dreams at the Fountain of Youth Ranch

David and I were a middle-aged couple when we decided it was time for us to live our lives the way we had dreamed and not by way of drifting.

In 2004, we heard about the unique Wine Route program of settling the Negev Area in the desert that makes up the largest part of the State of Israel, and we immediately decided to join in.

It was not easy: we were older-than-average urban people and did not fit the type the government was seeking to have as settlers on a chain of agritourism farms. On one hand, these farms were supposed to be an attraction for incoming tourism, and on the other, they were innovative model family farms using agricultural technology.

As active consulting lawyers, we knew nothing about either at the time, but did not give up, which is the motto of our lives and the only way we know. As second-generation Holocaust survivors, we learned determination and perseverance.

And that is how we were authorized and recognized as the fifth of twenty-three family agritourism farms on the Negev Wine Route.

We put on khaki pants and boots, left our "dreamy life" in Tel Aviv behind, and headed to the Negev. The spot we chose was not far from the main road, yet unseen from it. We had a dream and were unaware of what lay ahead. Israel was our one and only home, and this, the largest part of our country, was the least inhabited. If we could make a difference, we would!

To us, nature is the beginning and end of it all, a wonderful source for a simple, fulfilling, meaningful life, where time is an important dimension that you have to appreciate and not push, where seasons are to be respected and not changed, where soil is so rare that you learn to cherish it in this rocky area.

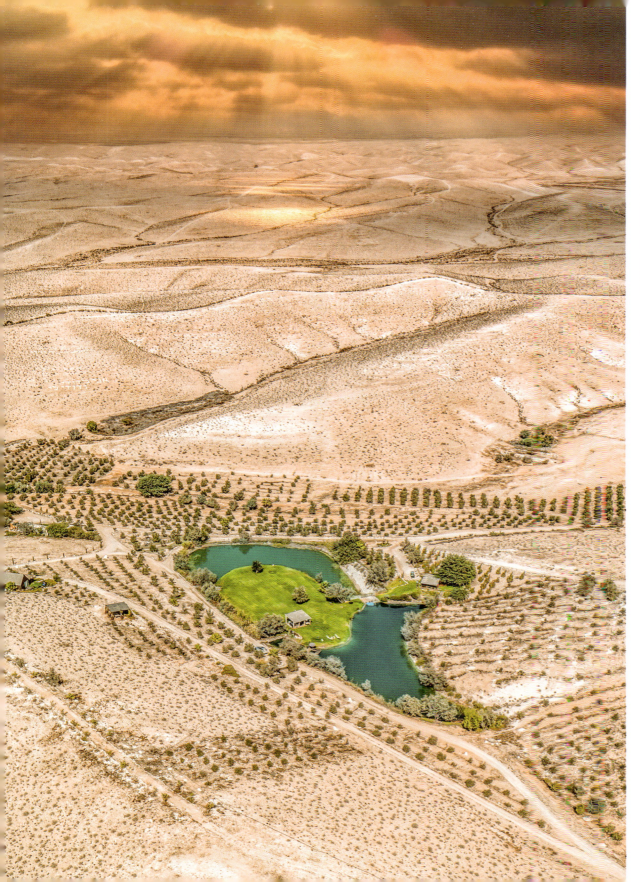

Indeed, it was hard work, yet very fulfilling and moreover somewhat mystical, just like the life of the Jewish people in Israel throughout history. Without everyday small miracles, we would not be where we are today.

When we were young, John Lennon encouraged us to dream with his song "Imagine." Later, President Shimon Peres challenged us in our long walking talks to "dream big" and "not be afraid to fly on the wings of your imagination." And it is David, my compañero for nearly fifty years, with whom I am realizing our mutual dream. Our Fountain of Youth is a state of mind coming to life in the desert.

We made the desert into an oasis by drawing water from an aquifer seven hundred meters underground, planting thirty-six hundred olive trees for future generations, creating a mini-habitat with water and pasture for animals of all kinds and migrating birds, a place for youngsters looking for a different way of life and for those seeking a peaceful place for the mind and soul.

Dreams, faith, determination, and perseverance are the symbols of our nation, and it is all represented in our Fountain of Youth in the Negev, Israel.

Chen Lichtenstein

The Desert Is Blooming in Neot Hovav

Chen Lichtenstein is Chief Financial Officer of the Syngenta Group, one of the world's leading agriculture companies. He was previously President and CEO at ADAMA, an industry leader in crop protection.

"It is in the Negev that the people of Israel will be tested – for only with a united effort … will we accomplish the great mission of populating the wilderness and making it flourish," wrote Israel's founding father, David Ben-Gurion, in a 1955 speech. He concluded with this seminal sentence: "This effort will determine the fate of the State of Israel and the standing of our people in the history of mankind."

Making the desert bloom embodied a combination of agriculture, industry, and sustainability. Close to seventy years later, as Highway 40 winds its way southward in the wilderness of the desert, we come upon the Neot Hovav eco-industrial park, which brings to life Ben-Gurion's inspiring vision. Seldom is a leader's vision embodied in the real world in such a precise and tangible way. The oasis-like site brings together nature's beauty and solitude with scientific advancement and the sustainable production of medication and food for mankind. It encapsulates, in a nutshell, the story of the revival of the State of Israel, which combines the realization of dreams of generations with forward-looking innovation.

Over the past decade and a half, I have been part of the journey of ADAMA, one of the world's leading crop protection and agricultural service providers, running the company and serving in a number of key positions. During this time, I witnessed the distinctive development of ADAMA as part of Neot Hovav, and the way the park has moved to the forefront of environmentally sustainable industry in Israel and worldwide.

While the State of Israel is not exceptionally rich in natural resources, it nurtures innovation and entrepreneurship, and it was out of the recognition of the human spirit of Israeli scientists and industrialists – and their ability to take risks to serve a greater purpose – that Neot Hovav was established. It was founded by people and for people.

Neot Hovav's enterprises don't include internet, media, or financial services, but rather pharmaceutical and agricultural concerns, as well as technology that advances sustainability and renewable energy, together forming a microcosm that addresses the most fundamental needs of people and nature. ADAMA, as well as other park participants, have established global R&D capabilities in Neot Hovav, drawing on and collaborating with some of Israel and the world's finest scientific minds.

Today, it is hard to imagine the Negev without Neot Hovav, which spans twenty thousand acres, generates growing economic benefits of more than $4 billion a year, and provides a living for eleven thousand families.

Medications, crop protection ingredients, and other scientific contributions of Neot Hovav reach millions of users across our planet and help transform their lives. The park itself marks a transformed way of manufacturing, which marries with the pristine desert landscape.

This can be seen in an aerial view of the region: in the heart of the desert bloom fields of solar energy panels and zero-discharge, environmentally friendly evaporation ponds larger than the industrial facilities.

For me, Neot Hovav represents one of the most profound realizations of Zionism and Israel's success. It translates Ben-Gurion's vision into a language of action, dealing with the most tangible challenges of our lifetime, through the start-up nation's ability to create something from nothing in the middle of the desert, harnessing courage, relentless resolve, inspiring talent, and a special connection to this land it seeks to preserve. And if it is in the Negev that the people of Israel are to be tested, Neot Hovav demonstrates that they're capable of taking on such a test, now and in the future.

Marcelle Machluf

Finding Home at the Dead Sea

Marcelle Machluf *is a Full Professor and the Dean of the Faculty of Biotechnology and Food Engineering at the Technion, as well as the director of the Laboratory for Cancer Drug Delivery and Cell Based Technologies. She received the Gutwirth Award for achievements in gene therapy, among other awards.*

Of all the beaches, deserts, valleys, and snow-capped peaks of our beautiful country, there is one place I cherish the most – the Dead Sea. For me, it represents home, a feeling that is deeply rooted in the memory of my mother, who loved this place dearly.

The beauty of the Dead Sea begins as soon as you enter the Judean Desert. Driving past the jagged mountains, you can feel the road descending toward the lowest body of water on earth. Hidden along the way are canyons carved over millennia by spring rains. Narrow sandstone wadis wait to be explored. At sunset, the crystallized water glitters red. Unlike the boisterous beaches of Tel Aviv or Haifa, the Dead Sea shore is spotted with quiet visitors anointed in black mud, floating peacefully in a sea of white and turquoise.

The first time I visited the Dead Sea, I was eight years old and giddy with excitement. I was on a camping trip with my mother and close family. Arriving at the sea, my first impression was of the strong smell of mud rich in bromine and its silky, oily texture. My aunt, who has been to the Dead Sea before, gave us a strong warning: "Always protect your eyes. Never put your entire head in the water." Moments later, my mother walked into the sea and plunged in. She came up screaming and kicking, spouting profanities I dare not repeat here. My aunt quickly ran for fresh water to pour over my mother's eyes. That evening, her eyes red and burning, my mother swore she would never go back. But the next morning, I found her calm and happy, floating in the water.

Set at the heart of the Rift Valley, the Dead Sea is a hiker's haven, perfect for anyone seeking the kind of quiet solitude only a desert can offer. Later on in my adult life, my mother and I used to make the hot, dry hikes through the beautiful canyons of Nahal David with its fantastic wildlife, visit the refreshing waterfalls and springs, or climb to Masada at sunrise to appreciate the Roman stronghold, remarkable evidence of ancient civilization. Many times, we camped at the Ein Gedi Reserve, a green oasis at the brown foothills east of the sea.

During those trips, my mother would often reminisce about the life she left behind. "This is just like the Ouzoud Falls back home in Morocco," she would say. She would tell me stories from her youth of how she spent long, hot days at the foot of the cascading falls surrounded by family and friends, placing watermelons in the water to cool them down.

My mother made aliyah to Israel in 1964, together with her mother and me, then an eighteen-month-old baby. While she regretted having to leave her home, she felt that Morocco was no longer a safe place for the Jewish people. She came to Israel believing the land of the Jews would offer an escape from the increasing persecution.

Unfortunately, my mother soon discovered that the reality of life in twenty-year-old Israel was not all she had hoped for. From a palace-like Moroccan home, she was now reduced to a two-bedroom apartment in Ashdod that could barely fit the dining table she had brought with her at great cost. A single mom in a foreign land, she struggled to find employment. Hearing Arabic spoken on the street was another shock, as was having to fend off discrimination and poor treatment as a Sephardic Jew.

Years later, when I visited Morocco, I finally understood why my mother found the Dead Sea so comforting. The land she left was blessed with glorious natural gems; the David Waterfall pales in comparison to the Ouzoud Falls. But to her, the landscape and the engulfing peace and quiet of the Dead Sea were a welcome reminder of her childhood. At the Dead Sea was where I got to see my mother truly happy.

Today, I visit the Dead Sea with my family at least once a year. Sadly, the sea has suffered unforgivable damage, primarily at the hands of conglomerates who have been pumping it for salt and minerals for years. By now, the southern basin has dried out, irreparably changing the physical appearance of the sea and causing sinkholes to pop up all along its shores. I consider myself fortunate to have had the chance to enjoy this timeless marvel, and I urge anyone who wishes to do the same to hurry before it tragically disappears from our world.

Sivan Yaari is the founder and CEO of Innovation: Africa, a nonprofit that has brought Israeli solar, agricultural, and water technologies to three million people across ten African countries. She holds a master's degree in energy from Columbia University. Sivan has received multiple awards, including the United Nations Innovation Award.

Sivan Yaari

Kalia: A Hopeful Landscape

At the northern tip of the Dead Sea, amidst the desolation of the Judean Desert, lies a small oasis called Kalia. It is neither world famous nor very well known among Israeli residents. It is more likely to be driven by or used as a rest stop on the way to the more familiar tourist resorts of the Dead Sea. But this is the place in Israel that most resonates with me.

It is a relatively remote outpost in the lowest place on earth sandwiched in the valley between the hills of Judea and the ridges of Jordan. Adjacent to the end of the Jordan River, Kalia is a meeting place between the sweet waters that flow from the Kinneret (Sea of Galilee) and the salty ones of the Dead Sea, the lowest-altitude body of water on earth.

It reflects the extreme contrast of the harshness of the Dead Sea Valley and the mirage of life-giving water. The raw beige hue of the exquisite layers of sand in the mountains against the deep turquoise of the Dead Sea are magnificent.

After traveling through the harsh, rugged dunes and forgotten caves, one arrives at a small and simple kibbutz, whose homes are fashioned in the shades of the terrain. There is nothing opulent or grandiose about the setting or the homes. It's just the simplicity of nature, without pretense.

I feel at peace there. The desert and rocky landscape remind me of the challenges and hardships the Jewish people faced in reclaiming and working our land just a century ago.

But beyond that, to me, Kalia represents hope and tranquility. It is that rare inflection point in nature, a stark reminder of critical moments we all face in our lives. The turmoil of barren and stingy soil gives way to a cluster of verdant palm trees. Here, in one of the bleakest of places, where one would think nothing could grow, are the sweetest of date fruits. The Medjool dates are as plump and rich with flavor as the desert in which they grow is barren.

The nearby uncrowded beach is pristine in its simple beauty. I descend into the salty waters of the Dead Sea and feel instantly alive. The sharp sting of the salty water burns all forgotten scratches and cuts. As I progress from the rocky beach into the sea, the water level rises. Just at the moment when you think your head will be submerged, your body flips on its side, and you find yourself floating, as if on an imaginary raft.

For me, Kalia is more than just a beautiful place – it is also a metaphor for my work with Innovation Africa. In countries in sub-Saharan Africa, we travel to the most remote regions, places with no running water or electricity where no tourists visit, places that are forgotten and offer little hope for progress.

It is precisely there that we go to share Israeli solar and water technology and provide the critical ingredients for economic development. I am constantly inspired by Israel's story of transforming the barren desert and marshy swamps into a flourishing agricultural zone, from a war-torn nation to a start-up nation. When I stop to imagine what progress and prosperity could be achieved with a population and area so much larger, sometimes the task seems far too daunting. It is then that I think of Kalia and am filled with hope.

Photo: Moses Pini Siluk

Dr. Aliza Bloch is the first female mayor of Beit Shemesh. A longtime educator, she holds a doctorate in education from Bar-Ilan University. She was previously Vice-Principal of Givat Gonen Elementary School in Jerusalem and Principal of Branco-Weiss High School in Beit Shemesh, as well as a tour guide.

Aliza Bloch

Tel Beit Shemesh: Beit Shemesh for All

Alongside Route 38, between the northern and southern entrances to the city of Beit Shemesh, there is a very special place that connects old with new, past with progress. It is a place that bridges worlds – Tel Beit Shemesh.

The tel occupies an area of 7.5 acres (30 dunams) and sits atop a hill 820 feet high (250 meters), at a strategic location on the Nachal Sorek riverbed from the north and Nachal Shemesh from the west. The first archeological excavations of this site were initiated in 1911 by the British Palestine Exploration Fund. In 1990, Tel Aviv University began excavations at the site.

The city of Beit Shemesh sits on the main road that runs between Jerusalem and Tel Aviv, an important location in terms of national planning. Beit Shemesh integrates tradition and innovation, past and present, and thus the city is a reflection of the tel.

As a resident of Beit Shemesh, I have visited the tel many times. Each visit takes me back to my days as a tour guide. While my fellow visitors to the site may prefer to focus on the view and are less interested in explanations, I feel the need to tell the story of this place once again, to connect between past and present.

Shortly after I became mayor, I was faced with a choice – to preserve the site's archeology and history, or to improve the traffic flow at the main junction at the city entrance. This beautiful place suffered much disruption. Both sides held demonstrations and protests.

We were asked to choose "either/or" – but I came to say "and." After a one-year delay, we decided that instead of paving a two-way road with four lanes, we would pave a two-way road with two lanes and build a bridge connecting the two sides of the tel. Neither side was satisfied. The tel would be divided, and we would have only two traffic lanes in each direction instead of four. But the value of maintaining unity and shared responsibility is stronger than any victory.

The lobby of the Beit Shemesh municipality is used for exhibits by local artists. Alongside the temporary exhibitions, there is a permanent display on Tel Beit Shemesh. Visitors interested in learning about the tel can come here and see archeological findings with photographs of the site and explanations. But I won't let you get away with merely reading about it. As a former tour guide and current mayor, I assure you that a visit to Tel Beit Shemesh is worthwhile all year round, but winter is a particularly good time. In January, you'll enjoy the bright red poppies along with many other blooms and plenty of shiny greenery. The visit to the tel is on a circular footpath that the entire family can enjoy, free of charge.

From the top of the tel, you can see the Beit Shemesh industrial zones, another angle of old versus new. The promotion of industry in the city creates waves that affect many other areas of life.

We host many visits to our city, by journalists, politicians, managers of high-tech companies, leaders of Israel's economy, and more. Tel Beit Shemesh features in many of these visits, including those unrelated to tourism.

Photo: Dr. Avishai Teicher Pikiwiki Israel (CC BY 2.5)

This is for several reasons – the rich and astonishing beauty of the site, as well as its symbolism of the encounter between new and old. Finally, the tel serves as a reminder to us all that the model of arrangement and agreement can be applied in other areas of conflict.

Soon, Beit Shemesh will work to develop tourism in the city. We plan to build a visitor center at the tel and a hotel and large sports park in the city. We are planning walking paths in the city that will serve diverse populations, as well as a virtual reality experience for tourists

I'll end by noting that a decade ago, excavations at the tel revealed a fingernail-sized seal with the figure of a man holding the head of an animal from the cat family. Do you know which Bible story this represents? And who was the first "mayor" of Beit Shemesh – do you know? In other words, you're all invited to come visit.

Brigadier General (Ret.) Dani Harari

Serving My Country in Re'ut

On entering Re'ut, visitors are greeted by a lovely avenue of ficus trees and purple booms of jacarandas, red and purple bougainvillea, and palm trees.

The surrounding hills are filled with groves of typical Mediterranean vegetation and abundant flowers: white squill and meadow saffron in the fall; daffodils, red anemones, and pink primroses in the winter; yellow chrysanthemums and red buttercups in the spring. Spice plants such as oregano, thyme, and sage emit a powerful scent. Herds of cows and sheep from the surrounding villages wander freely among the hills, escorted by a variety of birds. Each step in the fresh air of this landscape offers a deep experience of connection to the beauty of ever-changing nature.

The community of Re'ut is located in the Judean Hills inside the Green Line, in the middle of the road about half an hour east to Jerusalem and west to Tel Aviv. To the east, we can see the hills of Jerusalem and the Palestinian village of Beit Sira; to the west, the Mediterranean. The hills of Re'ut rise to a height of 720–1000 feet (220–300 meters).

The town of Re'ut was founded in 1983 in the area west of Maccabim. The IDF initiated the building project of small semi-attached private homes with red roofs. I was part of the founding community, with funding from members of the defense establishment. The goal of the project was to encourage young IDF personnel to remain in the military for long-term, permanent positions. To be accepted to the project, I signed a commitment for eight years of additional service, and this led to an extensive military career.

Brigadier General (Ret.) Dani Harari is the former Commander of Unit 8200, Israel's elite high-tech intelligence unit. He has served as Senior Vice President for Strategy Innovation and Resources at ADAMA Agricultural Solutions and is a partner in IL Ventures (ILVP Fund, LP).

Photos: Dani Harari

In 1990, Maccabim and Re'ut became one community. Today Re'ut has around sixteen hundred families and seven thousand residents. In 1996, the city of Modi'in was founded, and in 2003 the three communities were united into the city of Modi'in-Maccabim-Re'ut, with Maccabim and Re'ut preserving their rural and communal character as an independent neighborhood within the new city. Today Modi'in-Maccabim-Re'ut has about 100,000 residents, and the plan is for it to grow to 250,000 residents.

The city is named after the ancient settlement of Modi'in, home of the Hasmonean high priest Matityahu and his five sons from the biblical story of Chanukah. This town is also located in the Judean plain, east of Lod. Maccabim was the name given to Matityahu's sons, including Judah the Maccabee. The ancient settlement of Modi'in was apparently founded on top of a hill called Hamodi'im (the announcers), because from that peak, the residents would make announcements to the surrounding settlements using torches or smoke signals.

The city is sprinkled with many archeological sites from the Hasmonean period to the Ottoman period, including remains of agricultural settlements, oil and wine presses, and groves of almond, fig, and olive trees.

Re'ut is known nationwide for its outstanding educational system. Its students have a high percentage of matriculation in many subjects, and also one of the highest percentages of youth entering the IDF, as pilots and combat soldiers as well as in the intelligence and cyber units.

In Hebrew, the word *re'ut* means fellowship or friendship, as in the verse "You must love your fellow [*re'acha*] as yourself" (Leviticus 19:18), and indeed, many lasting friendships have arisen here. The first generation of children born on Re'ut have married, built their own families, and are returning to live here in Re'ut, Maccabim, or Modi'in.

When I came here with my wife Meirav over thirty years ago to visit the site where Re'ut would be built, we had to use our imaginations to envision how our home would look in the bare hills among the rocks and thorns. The strong sense of connection to this land and the opportunity to create and build something new in Israel overcame our doubts.

Looking back, this was a very significant decision in our lives. I was inspired by my grandfather, a farmer who made aliyah from Bulgaria. In 1929, he was one of the founders of Moshav Beit Hanan, where I was born and grew up.

I retired from the IDF at the rank of brigadier general, whose insignia is a crossed sword and olive branch. It has been my privilege to serve my country and to found a new settlement in the Land of Israel, in the hope of peace and friendship with our neighbors. That is the narrative of Zionism and the story of my Israel – Re'ut.

Adi Altschuler is a leader and an acclaimed social entrepreneur. She is the founder and CEO of Israel Inclusive schools, the founder of the youth organization Krembo Wings, and created Zikaron Basalon, an alternative Holocaust Memorial Day gathering.

Adi Altschuler

Always on the Way to Arsuf Beach

In the last twelve years of his life, the physician and Hebrew poet Shaul Tchernichovsky enjoyed the privilege of living in the land he had dreamed of his entire life – the Land of Israel. Five years after his death, the State of Israel was founded. Shaul never lived in the state, but he expressed his powerful love for this country in his poems.

In one of his well-known poems, he writes, "Man is nothing but the image of his native landscape."

In selecting the place that I love the most in my homeland, I feel that I'm being asked to look in the mirror and choose the image of the landscape that encapsulates me: Adi, the child, the woman, the wife, the mother, the social entrepreneur, the friend. But all these can't really be compressed into any landscape image.

Still, I think there is one place in Israel that contains me, a place where I really feel at home – one image of a landscape that represents me and connects me to my roots and to myself: Arsuf Beach. Don't feel bad if you haven't heard of it. Even the average Israeli doesn't know about this almost secret strip of coastline that's difficult to find. But those who persist and discover this hidden site will enjoy a rare glimpse into the essential meaning of my Israel – the Israel that I love so deeply, the Israel of giving, charity, love, helping others, of spirit and unlimited dreams, despite all the difficulties that surround us.

To tell the truth, I deliberated over whether to share this secret with you, because I don't want this place to become a public site. I wouldn't want thousands of tourists to come rushing to this little slice of the divine. As yet, few know of its existence, but if you won't pass this secret on and it remains only mine and yours, then I'm willing to share.

So first of all, I'll tell the story of Arsuf Beach, and then I'll explain how to find this hidden piece of Eden.

This isn't a developed beach. There aren't any lifeguards here, or beach chairs or umbrellas, or white sand or palm trees. It's hard to reach – you have to make an effort to get here. This means that the beach operates a natural filter system, allowing entrance only to those who really want to be here. It's visited by many Israelis who have been to India to clear their minds and miss the spiritual atmosphere, wanna-be hippies, sixties lovers, but mainly just people who love this place. And it returns their love.

Other beaches might be more beautiful, but no beach shares its particular beauty.

This beach has atmosphere. A frequency.

The Arsuf and Ga'ash cliffs surround it on all sides and leave a relatively small and compact strip of magic.

Here we find a boat submerged in the water that divers visit on occasion, and small, gorgeous lagoons alongside sharp, jagged rocks.

This is why it's so Israeli to me. Like the sabras that are spiny on the outside but soft in the middle, this beach seems rocky and abandoned. But when you get to know it, when you sit here for a moment and breathe in the atmosphere, when you listen to the whisper of the waves and what lies underneath them, then you discover its charm.

Of course, I'm biased. My best memories lie there on a faded beach towel. In some years, I was there every Saturday. When I was sad and when I was happy, when things were difficult and lonely, when I celebrated with friends.

In every mood and on any day this beach welcomed me with open arms. It stroked my hair and embraced me with love. But I'm sure that it will welcome you with a hug, too, and it will return your love generously.

So how do we get there? Take Route 2 to the environmental statue park at Arsuf Kedem and go past the hills and open spaces of the nature reserve. Park there, then walk down to the small, wild beach.

If you decide to make the effort and find my secret beach, say hi for me and tell it that Adi's on the way. I'm always on the way there.

Gilad Sharon holds an MA in agricultural economics and management from the Hebrew University of Jerusalem. Author of the bestselling biography Sharon: The Life of a Leader about his father, Prime Minister Ariel Sharon, he lives on and manages the family's Shikmim Farm and serves as a major in reserve duty in an elite IDF unit.

Gilad Sharon

Kfar Malal and the Long-Gone Casuarina Trees

If you drive from Hod Hasharon to Raanana and get distracted for just a second, you'll miss Kfar Malal without even noticing. The houses of the moshav where my father was born were built flanking the road, which was only a dirt track at the time. Over the years, more and more cars traveled the road, and it grew like a snake, until it reached monstrous proportions and swallowed up most of the moshav.

The word *moshav* conjures up the image of a pastoral site in the midst of fields. Not Kfar Malal. It went from being in the countryside to being hemmed in by the cities that grew up around it, sliced through by busy highways.

Its land became prime real estate. Many people would be happy to live there. When the Iraqi army was on its doorstep, when it was being raided by Arab gangs and the residents had to dig trenches to defend themselves, it was less desirable.

It was while they were digging one of those trenches that my grandparents found the skull of a Turkish soldier from World War I. We called him McGregor.

"Did you have anything to do with his death?" I asked.

"He was a Turkish soldier who died in the war."

If your grandmother tells you she didn't kill him, she didn't kill him. But it's not as if she wasn't capable of dispatching a few McGregors if she wanted to.

My grandparents, Vera and Samuil, settled in Kfar Malal in November 1922. They lived in a tent for a year and a half before moving to a two-room shack they built with their own hands: one room for them and the other for the cow and the mule. Sometime later, a concrete cowshed was constructed, and the animals' living conditions improved

Vera and Samuil with Arik, Kfar Malal, early 1930s (from the family album)

Arik Sharon and his sister Dita on the casuarina-lined street in Kfar Malal, early 1930s (from the family album)

substantially. My grandparents remained in the cabin, where Dita and Arik, my aunt and my father, were born.

The members of the moshav were strong and stubborn. They held on tenaciously to the red soil of the Sharon district, bringing water in a barrel from the Yarkon River with a horse-drawn wagon and living under the constant threat of terror attacks. But there were a few special characters among them who added color to their hard life. One was known as a straight arrow and was therefore chosen to mark the boundaries of the members' plots. He walked with a limp, one leg longer than the other. When it turned out that his plot was bigger than the others, he explained, "I measured mine with my long leg." And who can forget the man who couldn't stop himself from taking Vera's newspaper every morning. They eventually came to an agreement that satisfied both sides: Vera got today's paper and left yesterday's in her mailbox for him to steal.

Vera had studied medicine in Russia for four years. She dreamed of completing medical school here. When she arrived in this desolate land, she realized there was no education to be had. In fact, there was nothing here at all. Samuil was an outstanding agronomist. He was highly educated, devoured books, painted, and played the violin. He passed away at the young age of sixty. Left alone, Vera tended the exemplary farm on her own for many years.

She had high cheekbones and almond-shaped eyes. Although she wasn't tall, she was tough and very strong, both physically and mentally. I imagined her as a product of Genghis Khan's campaigns. Thousands of Mongolian soldiers galloping on their small horses for weeks or months across the vast Russian steppes – short, rugged, and determined, their almond eyes narrowed against the wind. Nothing deters them; no one can stop them. Beneath them, between the saddle and the horse's back, they keep a ration of meat that is cured by the friction and the sweat of the animal. All this came to mind whenever I saw my beloved grandmother.

There once was a long, majestic row of seventy-year-old casuarina trees. They were the pride of Kfar Malal and the symbol of the moshav. They, too, were swallowed up by the accursed road.

Ido Schoenberg and Phyllis Gotlib

Peace on Mount Tavor

We live in a tiny village in the lower Galilee called Kfar Kisch. It is the place we call home. It's best to enjoy the view from our terrace while sampling the exceptionally delicious yet simple local cuisine. We make our own oil, wine, hummus, and bread. Who needs more?

Our little paradise features small hills that change every day to reflect nature's cycles. The fields are filled with life. Birds grace the skies while cattle bells chime across the valley. The call of the muezzin from faraway mosques melds with church bells in the distance.

Olives and almonds dominate the scene together with vines and oak trees. On February mornings, the sun paints the almond flowers bright white and flaming pink. We breathe the cool, sweet air and fall in love with our place again.

We never get tired of looking at our view of Mount Tavor, its perfect shape – rising starkly from the gently sloping land that surrounds it – silhouetted by amazing sunsets.

The Hebrew name of our mountain is Tavor – a word close to *tabor* (navel). On clear nights, when the Church of Transfiguration on the mountaintop is lit up and the stars shine bright, we can almost feel the umbilical cord that reconnects us with our land. The special topography creates a microclimate that promises a much-needed breeze every afternoon – even on the hottest of summer days. You can see and hear the wind dancing in the wheat and trees.

If you climb up the mountain, you see a piece of Israel.

The valley right under you is part of Via Maris, an ancient passage from the Jezreel Valley northward toward Damascus. This is the place where Sisera led a Canaanite army against

Ido Schoenberg, MD, is Chairman and CEO of Amwell and oversees the company's corporate strategy. In 1996, together with Phyllis Gotlib, he cofounded iMDSoft, a provider of enterprise software that automates hospital critical care units.

Phyllis Gotlib is the President of Amwell International. She also serves as an executive partner in Flare Capital Partners, supporting diversified investments in digital health portfolio companies. Prior to Amwell, Phyllis founded and led iMDsoft, a global leader in critical care automation.

the Israelites. It is also where Deborah – the Jewish prophetess – summoned Barak of the tribe of Naphtali to fight back and change history.

The villages that you see were home to the founding fathers of Israel. From Ben-Gurion to Peres, from Rabin to Yigal Alon, they all spent years breathing the local air that shaped their love and dedication to our country.

The magnificent vista is a unique collage. Fertile land is dressed in endless shades of green. Jewish and Arab villages are scattered all around. You can see the abrupt transition into the desert. The lights of the holy cities of Nazareth and Safed blend with those of Jordanian cities across the river.

The occasional roar of a jet fighter heading north may serve as a crude wake-up call to the complex reality that has been the hallmark of our piece of paradise over the millennia. You may be overwhelmed by thousands of years of history. You may be stunned by the impossible diversity of scents, sounds, and sights. And yet, it all converges into a surprising tranquility, as if an unexpected equilibrium is finally established.

There are crisper days in New England and higher mountains in Switzerland. The magic of Israel is in the measure of mercy. Nothing is too much or too little, and everything is treasured. It is a perfect imperfection.

Photos: Gil Shwed

PART III

Ofra Strauss

The Music of Coexistence in Akko

The city of Akko holds a special place in the hearts of the Strauss family and company. As a family, we have a strong connection to the city as my grandparents and father immigrated to the nearby town of Nahariya and founded the family's ice cream business in Akko. Growing up, I spent a lot of time exploring the city which has a rich history. The Old City is a UNESCO World Heritage Site and one of the oldest ports in the world. The city's history and architecture have been shaped by various cultures and civilizations, including the Romans, Byzantines, Crusaders, Muslims, Mamelukes, Ottomans, and the British Empire.

Akko is a shining example of coexistence, with a diverse population made up of Jews, Christians, and Muslims. The vibrant market in Akko, with its diverse offerings and mix of cultures, is a microcosm of the city and country as a whole. One of my favorite places in the city is the Strauss Music Conservatory, founded by my father in honor of my grandparents and as a symbol of music's ability to bring people together.

As a child, I always knew the importance of food to people's lives. More than a basic need, food brings us together and enables us to express who we are. This is evident in Akko's market: one of the most diverse, colorful, and exciting markets in Israel, it is also the beating heart of the city. In it, you can find amazing hummus, spices and herbs, Arab sweets, specialty pots and pans, clothes, and even toys, but the market is so much more than its stalls and shops. It is a symphony of coexistence and reflects what Israel is all about – a place that Jews, Muslims, Christians, and many others consider holy and call home. A place where one's faith and beliefs are respected, a place where all can celebrate and enjoy their own culture and that of their neighbors.

Ofra Strauss is Chairperson of the Strauss Group, Israel's second-largest food and beverage company. She previously held positions in Estée Lauder International and on the Supervisory Board of Royal Numico. She founded Catalyst Israel for the promotion of women in business and chaired Maala, which promotes corporate citizenship and social responsibility.

Photo: Avraham Graicer (CC BY-SA 4.0)

Being in the market and experiencing its vibrancy – surrounded by the aroma of the shops, hearing the muezzin's call to prayer from the mosques and the sounds of the sea – feels like you are taking part in the concert of life. This experience is what led my father to put all his love and energy into the city of Akko after he retired from managing the Strauss Group. The city and its development became his mission in life. The conservatory is a product of his love for the city, its people, and music.

I believe that my father's wish in building the Strauss Municipal Conservatory in honor of his parents was to commemorate them in a place where Jews and Arabs come together and celebrate life and the idea of coexistence through music. It was founded on the belief that music brings people together. Today I see that his wish came true: the conservatory is home to more than 750 students from all faiths, where children of all ages learn, strive for excellence, and express themselves through music.

When inaugurating the conservatory, my father said, "I want to thank the people of Akko for giving me something I never thought possible: getting back more than you give. There is so much satisfaction knowing that from a place that has suffered so many conflicts and trouble, we will grow a community that flourishes together, overcoming prejudice and racial injustice, and make a real change." To me, this is our legacy, not only in Akko but all over the country, both as a society and as a company. There is nowhere better to witness the potential of our country than Akko.

Akko – Ofra Strauss

Imad Telhami is Founder and Chairman of Babcom Centers. He was previously CEO of the Delta Galil textile company. He also founded and chairs a venture capital firm, Takwin (Arabic for "Genesis").

Imad Telhami

Finding Strength Together in Haifa

It is hard to separate all the things that make up who I am. I am an Arab, an Israeli, a Christian raised in a village where the majority is Druze but where Muslims and Jews live as well. To some, this may sound challenging. But I made a decision long ago to embrace every part of my diverse identity, with all its inner contradictions and obstacles, thus turning apparent weaknesses into strengths.

The place where all of this comes together for me is Babcom (Arabic for "Your Gateway"), the service company that I created ten years ago motivated by a drive to combine business and social mission. Babcom was created as a place where diversity is a natural state of being, where women and men, religious and secular, Arabs, Muslims, Druze, Christians, and Jews work together and find common ground in a hub of coexistence.

Two powerful experiences have shaped my perspective on Israel, my identity, and my role as an Israeli citizen, eventually leading to the birth of Babcom. The first has to do with the struggles I experienced early on in my career as one of the first Arab executives to join a company made up of exclusively Jewish management. I was seen as the Other. Some even tried to have me removed from my position. But empowered by a supportive upper management, I chose to stay the course and rose to become CEO. Many years later, as I was getting ready to leave the company, my colleagues argued vocally for my retention.

The second experience was working for Dov Lautman, an Israeli luminary who chaired Israel's largest textile company, Delta Galil. Dov became a mentor, a father figure, and a role model. He did not see me as the Other but as a talented human being and fellow Israeli. In a sense, the idea of Babcom was born here, in a place that transcends difference, empowers, and inspires.

I left Delta with a pressing mission: to close the economic gap between Arabs and Jews and bring more minority groups into the fold of the "start-up nation." It pained me that Arab women, many with college degrees, had the

Sderot Ben Gurion and the German Colony (photo: Grauesel [CC BY-SA 3.0])

View from the Bahá'í Gardens (photo: Steven Kolins)

highest unemployment rate in the Middle East. Other communities such as the ultra-Orthodox Jews, Bedouins, and Druze were also being left behind.

And so Babcom was born, quickly becoming everything I hoped it would be and much more. Today, it is a diverse home to more than three thousand employees, 60 percent of whom are Arab and 78 percent women. Here, we all work side by side, Christians and Muslims, Druze and ultra-Orthodox Jews, Ethiopians and Russians. In 2011, Babcom was acquired by Matrix, Israel's leading technology services company, thus becoming the first Arab start-up to complete a successful exit.

Today, Babcom has twelve locations, spanning peripheral Israel from south to north. The headquarters is located at the entrance to Migdal Tefen, overlooking beautiful views of the Upper Galilee. Like all of Babcom's offices, the location was deliberately chosen to promote an equilibrium between center and periphery.

Migdal Tefen, built in 1980, is the first industrial council in Israel. Its center is a highly developed industrial park with over sixty factories. Like Babcom, it is a model of diversity, with employees coming from the surrounding towns and villages, including Druze, Christians, Muslims, and Jews. The Tefen Open Museum offers a unique combination of industry, art, and heritage and is well worth the visit.

The German Colony, Haifa (photo: StateofIsrael [CC BY-SA 2.0])

Babcom is the place that inspires me the most. In 2014, it inspired me to found Takwin Ventures, a venture capital firm that strives to help Arab entrepreneurs be part of the "start-up nation" by making early-stage investments in start-up companies that involve an Arab-Israeli entrepreneur. The Haifa-based fund invests in groundbreaking technologies, and its companies employ over two hundred people, both Arabs and Jews. It isn't only the mission that has been gratifying; it is also the Arab-Jewish partnership in making it happen – especially the partnership with my dedicated friends Chemi Peres and Erel Margalit..

Noam Gershony

Growing Community at Bustan Thom (Thom's Orchard)

Thom's Orchard is a special place tied closely to my heart, my beliefs, and my values. The orchard, called Bustan Thom in Hebrew, was established in 2010 as an educational center promoting coexistence between man and nature and the importance of sustainability.

Bustan Thom is named after my good friend Captain Thom Farkas, an Apache helicopter pilot who died on July 24, 2006, during the Second Lebanon War. He was on his way back from a mission to stop a Hezbollah terrorist cell bombing civilian territories in Israel when his helicopter malfunctioned and crashed. It happened while I was unconscious and hospitalized due to my own injury, and I learned about his death three days after I woke up. Hearing the news of his death was the hardest, most heartbreaking moment of my life. He was only twenty-three years old and had a unique kind soul. In his memory and spirit, his family decided to follow his path and invest in the existence and sustainability of Israel.

The mission of Thom's Orchard is to spotlight the importance of agriculture and nature as the foundations of our existence. It also advocates volunteering and contribution to one's community and country. The place is built as a small farm that reconnects its visitors to the land and the origins of the food we put on our plates. It showcases solutions for growing food without using pesticide that were developed here in Israel.

All the trees, vines, and plants in the orchard were planted by family, friends, and volunteers who continue to maintain the orchard and its crops on a daily basis.

Photo: Razi Livnat

Noam Gershony, *a former Israeli Air Force pilot, suffered devastating injuries in his own helicopter crash days before the crash that killed Thom Farkas during the 2006 Lebanon War. He is a gold medal–winning wheelchair tennis player.*

The educational center has ten different activities from the world of agriculture, farm culture, and sustainability. Each station gives the visitor hands-on experience in different topics such as soil cultivation, water purification, air pollution, and more. The stations model creative ecological solutions to different environmental issues and are meant to inspire and educate visitors to take part in the environmental revolution and support public health and sustainable development.

The Bustan is open for the general public to come and enjoy its beautiful garden and activities. It hosts over five thousand guests from a variety of backgrounds: schoolchildren from kindergarten through high school, military units, professional organizations, families, private visitors, and guests from abroad.

The orchard has been inspired by the values of the worldwide organic movement that mirror the legacy of Thom and all those who have given their lives for our existence:

- Health
- Ecology
- Fairness
- Care and personal responsibility

Thom gave his life for the State of Israel and for the Jewish nation. Knowing him, he did not have any second thoughts; he was always the first to volunteer and put his life at risk in order to help protect the citizens of Israel. His amazing spirit lives through the orchard in the connection between the land and its people.

Thom's Orchard - Noam Gershony

Maysa Halabi Alshekh

Higher High Tech on Mount Carmel

Daliyat al-Karmel on Mount Carmel is the largest Druze village in Israel, home to the Muhraqa Monastery, where according to tradition "fire descended from the heavens." Here you will find the Oliphant House, site of the creation of the national anthem "Hatikvah," now serving as the Druze Memorial Center to commemorate the Druze soldiers who fell in Israel's wars. Other features of the village are enchanting nature views and Lotus, the first high-tech space for women in Israel's Arab and Druze society.

In Druze villages, most women excel in their studies, yet their employment opportunities are very limited, because by tradition, Druze women cannot drive, nor may they study or work in mixed-gender environments. Usually, they work for small local businesses at wages far below minimum. Religious Druze women have been forced to choose between high-paying work and their religious tradition and community.

I asked myself: Why should things be this way? By researching the job market, I learned that there was a real possibility for women to penetrate the world of programming, working remotely. If companies are hiring people from diverse cultures around the globe, why not us?

My vision was this: if we cannot make it to high tech, let us bring high tech to us. My mission was to grant women hope and the right to dream, to be independent and to take part in the "start-up nation," the Israeli innovation arena, as true partners in Israeli society.

My dream met those of fourteen other religious women who agreed to come on the journey with me. In the beginning, we met weekly at my parents' home; later, my in-laws donated their old house to us, and we spent about eighteen months there.

We broadcast our dream far and wide and met many people who believed in the importance of our project and

Maysa Halabi Alshekh is an educator, education and social entrepreneur, and founder and CEO of the Lotus space for women in high tech, an initiative to promote the employment of Druze and Arab women by making quality training and workplaces available in the social and geographic periphery.

in the true need to give equal opportunities to disadvantaged populations in Israeli society. One of the best people we met was Rami Schwartz, managing director of the Portland Trust in Tel Aviv. Our goal matched theirs: employment for underrepresented groups, equality, and social mobility. Rami and the trust immediately came on board to support the initiative.

We founded the Lotus NGO in 2018 to provide appropriate training and employment to talented women. For the first time in the history of Druze society, traditional women are given the opportunity to take on a significant part in supporting their families, improving the status of women and raising the proportion of women developers in Arab society in general, which today is at a mere 0.5 percent of the entire high-tech industry!

Our women are trained as full stack developers in an eight-month bootcamp combined with on-the-job training, then employed in remote positions at leading companies, working from the Lotus hub. The participants acquire skills necessary for the high-tech world, such as independent learning, teamwork, handling criticism and failure, soft skills, creativity, and business acumen.

After the first cohort graduated and the first group of candidates got hired, we requested the blessing and support of the highest Druze religious authority, Sheikh Mowafaq Tarif. This supreme spiritual leader blessed our initiative, saying that in the past, women used to work in textile factories, but now that the factories have moved to the east, Lotus will answer the women's survival needs while preserving identities.

Photos: Jinan Halabi

A year later, together with the entire world, we encountered COVID-19. All of a sudden, the remote work approach we pioneered with employers became a global reality: one can work anywhere, any time. Not a single one of our developers lost her livelihood, and in many cases, they became the main supporters of their families following layoffs in various sectors.

By the end of 2022, seventy-two women were employed as full stack developers in top-notch companies such as Amdocs, Radcom, Finastra, Algosec, Sapians, Incredibuled, Seetree, Identify, Abra, and Cloudedge. In 2023–2024, the second women's hub will open to serve the population of the Galilee. Lotus encompasses religious and nonreligious, Druze, Muslim, and Christian developers; the team includes a diversity of religions and is a true testament to Israeli hope.

Throughout the journey, I have felt enormously embraced and supported by all levels of Israeli society, including many philanthropic foundations, government bodies, commercial companies, communities, businesspeople, and volunteers from all over Israel. We invite you as well to become part of Lotus's circle of influence and support.

Lotus began as a localized solution to the needs of the Druze community, but today, it is a model for all communities and a kind of microcosm for Israeli society, proving that it is possible to understand and respect each other, all the while preserving individuality.

Such is our Israel, the "start-up nation," the country combining so many identities, so many conflicts, so many differences, but so much good. Lotus is a small example of Israeli social solidarity in doing good for the country and all its people. This is my Israel.

Hana Rado

Encounters, Connections, and Opportunities at Beit Harishonot

Hana Rado *is a social business entrepreneur who dedicates her life to promoting gender balance and to advancing occupational growth in Israel's remote peripheries. She is Founder and Chairperson of Group 19 and Founder and President of Supersonas.*

No photograph can adequately capture the beautiful view from the balcony of Beit Harishonot (Women Founders' House). From this point, the highest in the region, we see the entire eastern side of Emek Hefer beneath us. Thanks to the pleasant breeze from the ocean, we can sit outside and enjoy this breathtaking sight, even on hot summer days.

Beit Harishonot is a newcomer to the landscape of the Emek Hefer regional council. It opened on January 1, 2021, as a center for independently employed businesswomen to create connections and spark unique opportunities. It is located in a small, pastoral structure next to the historic Beit Harishonim (Founders' House), an old stone building that housed the founding group of Kfar Vitkin in the early 1930s. For many years, the charming wooden hut next to Beit Harishonim stood abandoned and neglected. But with the assistance and encouragement of Dr. Galit Shaul, head of the Emek Hefer local council, I decided to team up with another entrepreneurial woman, interior designer Michal Savion-Kushmaro, to transform this site into a meeting place for independently employed women in the region.

After a long, successful career in advertising, I decided to make a change in my life and became a social business entrepreneur. I established the Nineteen Group – social business entrepreneurs who are creating hundreds of new, quality jobs for women in Israel's peripheral areas. In 2015, I founded Supersonas, an apolitical social business initiative that overcomes communal barriers and acts to create a balancing female presence at intersections of influence and decision, both in Israel and globally.

My partner in this venture, Michal Savion-Kushmaro, was a successful, independently employed interior designer. Like me, she decided to change direction in her professional life. Inspired by our shared dream of social entrepreneurship, we became close friends. We wanted to work together to create a space where independently employed women could meet to create connections and spark opportunities – just as our own first encounter had done.

In 2019, we submitted our proposal to the Emek Hefer local council to renovate the abandoned hut in Emek Hefer and transform it into a center for independently employed women. We overcame many hurdles along the way, until finally, the official opening of Beit Harishonot was held last January.

The renovation of the hut was planned, managed, and physically implemented by the talented Michal, who proved her ability to transform the impossible into a reality. Beit Harishonot opened in the midst of the COVID-19 epidemic, between Israel's second and third lockdown, not exactly an ideal time for a new business. But despite the initial challenges, we managed to achieve our dream and hold an extensive program of quality activities at Beit Harishonot.

Even after Israel underwent another lockdown, a war, and another election, Beit Harishonot continued fulfilling our vision of encounters, connections, and opportunities. Throughout the day, the small hut serves as a shared workspace for women from all over the country, hosting networking events that enable personal and business opportunities. In the evenings, the space serves as a venue for courses that fit our agenda of women's empowerment (I call myself a "practical feminist"), such as financial planning for women, Supersonas school for future CEOs, and a unique accelerator program that offers tools for success to women in the early stages of founding a start-up. As part of our holistic, communal view, Beit Harishonot also offers cultural events, wine tastings, and professional development workshops.

We invite you to come visit!

Joey Low

Opportunity at Reichman University (IDC Herzliya)

Set in the heart of the bustling city of Herzliya is the Interdisciplinary Center (now Reichman University), Israel's first private university. The IDC has been a personal blessing for me. Over the years, I have found it to be an amazing institution whose Zionist vision matches my own, and together we accomplish great things.

My love story with Israel begins with my family history. I was born in New York in 1951. My parents, together with their families, had arrived in America during the Holocaust, both at the age of fifteen. My father's family came from Vienna. My mother, originally from Berlin, had lived for seven years in Belgium, then traveled to France and to Cuba before arriving in New York Harbor on Halloween in 1941.

My siblings and I went to Ramaz, a Modern Orthodox yeshiva on the Upper East Side of Manhattan. I attended the day school for twelve years, during which time I developed a strong connection to Jewish traditions and a special attachment to Israel. As a junior in college studying at NYU, I joined an exchange program at the Hebrew University of Jerusalem, an experience that changed my life.

During that year in Israel, I fell in love with the country and its people. One year later, during the Yom Kippur War, I came back as a volunteer to support the many friends I had made at college who'd been called back to join their units in the army to fight. The time I spent volunteering cemented my relationship with Israel. After the war, I returned to the United States, but my heart remained in Israel. I became active doing whatever I could to promote Israel and later, together with my wife, Carol, became active in the Jewish community

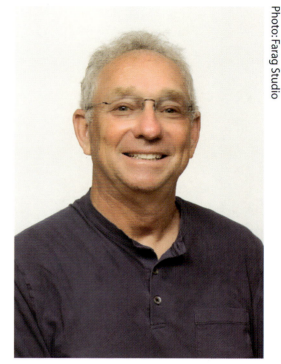

Joey Low is the founder of Israel at Heart and Star Farm Ventures, a venture capital firm supporting Israeli start-ups. He and his wife Carol, who made aliyah three years ago, have been longtime supporters of Reichman University (IDC Herzliya).

In 2002, when the IDF responded to a spate of horrific terror attacks with Operation Defensive Shield, I was frustrated by international criticism of Israel's policies, by the disparity between the images of Israel I saw in the media and the vibrant country I knew. I decided to take action, and it was at that point that I started Israel at Heart, and my relationship with the IDC began.

Israel at Heart was created to counter the media's negative portrayal of Israel and to promote a better understanding of Israel and its people. The idea was to send young Israelis who had just finished their army service to speak on college campuses across America. I believed that face-to-face encounters with young, eloquent IDF veterans would allow the public to form a more accurate impression of Israel. I provided the vision and funding, and many of the students I selected attended the IDC. The first few trips were very successful, and soon I was sending delegations all over the United States, Europe, and South America.

From the very beginning of the program, I insisted that each group of three students include members who spoke the local language of the country we were visiting and at least one Ethiopian Israeli, so that audiences could see the diversity of Israeli society and so we could address charges being made by some that Israel was an apartheid state. A meaningful result for me was that I became familiar with the Ethiopian community and grew to appreciate the tremendous contribution its members made and could make to Israeli society if given the opportunities other Israelis received.

And so in 2006, I approached Professor Uriel Reichman, IDC's president, with an offer to start a scholarship program exclusively for Ethiopian Israelis. He immediately agreed. The criteria I set were very good English, distinguished army service, and strong leadership qualities. We began with six students and added fifteen more each year after that. Today, the scholarship program has over fifty current students studying and over two hundred fifty graduates, many of whom are contributing to Israeli society in ways that go far beyond anything we could have hoped for.

In 2010, the IDC suggested I meet a few African asylum seekers who wanted to study at the university. When I met the first six candidates, their stories instantly reminded me of my parents, who had escaped Europe; these Africans had escaped genocide in Darfur and lifetime army conscription in Eritrea. I had always promised myself that if given the chance, I would try to help refugees live a more normal life with opportunities my parents weren't given in Europe nor even when they arrived in America. I immediately agreed to add the African students to my program. Today, we have over sixty graduates from Sierra Leone, Somalia, the Ivory Coast, Nigeria, South Sudan, Darfur, and Eritrea, as well as participants with student visas from Zambia and Rwanda.

For me, the IDC is where Israel is seen at its best. Formerly, this campus was an army base. Today, the tranquil atmosphere, broad lawns, and fountains enhance the innovative teaching facilities, offering better opportunities for our students to grow and contribute to the vibrant economy and Israeli society. I strongly recommend touring the campus to see Zionism and entrepreneurship flourishing.

Photo: Reichman University

Eytan Stibbe

A Message of Unity from Kiryat Adam, Lod

Kiryat Adam is an academic-psychotherapeutic treatment center, based on the principles of Human Spirit. It is located in Lod, a city steeped in spirituality.

The center focuses on training therapists and providing psychotherapeutic treatment to Lod's broad population. The center is located inside a renovated Brutalist-style school building that was built in the 1960s. The renovation, planned by Gottesman Szmelcman Architecture, is surrounded by a blossoming garden with a sitting area and intertwining paths that invite visitors for a peaceful, calm stroll. The guiding vision of the center is to train psychotherapists by offering them a broad, diverse education including humanities and Buddhism to enable quality psychological treatment for residents of Lod and the surrounding area.

In 1954, the Japanese people gifted to the United Nations a Peace Bell made from the coins of the sixty member nations. Some twenty countries worldwide have replicas of the World Peace Bell, and I had one brought to Kiryat Adam, where each year it is rung together with others around the world on September 21, International Peace Day.

The treatment center and the World Peace Bell represent the concept that we are all one human tapestry. The purpose of these two structures is to strengthen the inherent potential of Lod and transform it into a symbol of unity between members of different religions, to benefit all of the residents of this city that ranks three out of ten on the socioeconomic scale. The average income of its residents is one-fourth of Israel's national average, and a relatively low number of its high school graduates attain the matriculation certificate.

Photo: Elad Malka

Eytan Stibbe *is one of the founders of Kiryat Adam, an academic-psychotherapeutic treatment center. As an impact investor, he worked extensively in developing countries, mainly in Africa. In 2022, as Israel's second astronaut, he embarked on the seventeen-day Rakia Mission to the International Space Station.*

World Peace Bell installation by Num Stibbe at Kiryat Adam, Lod

Lod was the largest city in the region, before Modi'in and Shoham were built. Located in central Israel, near the airport, Lod has an impressive history. In the past, it was on the route that pilgrims took from Jaffa to Jerusalem, whether for purposes of peace or for war. The center of the city hosts houses of worship for three religions, reflecting coexistence and unity among the residents.

Lod is thirty-five hundred years old, which makes it one of the most ancient cities in Israel and perhaps even the entire world. In October 2009, the World Monuments Fund listed Lod as one of ninety-three endangered world heritage sites. It is the only city in Israel that was occupied in every one of the archeological and historical periods. Remnants were found there of a settlement from the New Stone Age, as well as from the Bronze Age (3500–1150 BCE) and the subsequent Iron Age. The Bible mentions Lod in I Chronicles (8:12), indicating that during the reign of King Yoshiyahu, members of the tribe of Benjamin lived there. The Sages relate that Lod was surrounded by a wall during the time of Joshua (Babylonian Talmud, *Megillah* 4a). The Book of Ezra (2:33) says that residents of Lod were exiled after the destruction of the First Temple in 586 BCE and eventually went back during the return to Zion. A century later, Lod appeared as one of the cities that obeyed Nehemiah's instruction to send representatives to strengthen Jerusalem.

The historical importance of the Jewish settlement in Lod is paralleled by the long Arab history of the city. This began during the ancient Arab (Muslim) period in Palestine. Arab

tribes under the caliphs Abu Bakar and Umar invaded Palestine and Syria from Hejaz, soundly defeating the Byzantine armies in 641. The caliphate continued for five hundred years until the Crusaders conquered Jerusalem in 1099. Palestine was again Muslim during the late Arab period, until the establishment of the State of Israel in 1948. The roots of Christianity in the city also run very deep. During the Byzantine period, most of the city's residents were Christian. So Lod is truly a city of three religions.

Today, the three faiths reside side by side in Lod's Peace Park. The Church of St. George the Dragon Slayer is of great importance to Greek Orthodox and Armenian Orthodox Christians. It was originally constructed during the Byzantine period and destroyed and rebuilt several times, until the current structure was built in the nineteenth century. The El Amri Mosque was built and dedicated during the late thirteenth century, while the youngest resident of the park is Sha'arei Shamayim Synagogue.

Passersby are invited to visit, ring the Peace Bell, visit the nearby historical sites of Lod, and experience the diamond in the rough that is hidden within this special city.

Photo: Yael Ayalon

Yuvi Tashome-Katz is the CEO and cofounder of Friends by Nature, an Israeli NGO founded primarily by young Israelis of Ethiopian descent. Her long, perilous journey to Israel through the Sudan desert in 1984 at the age of seven was featured in the children's book Yuvi's Candy Tree, available in Hebrew and in English.

Yuvi Tashome-Katz

An Ethiopian Story in Gedera

It is twilight, and the sun is reddening and setting on the horizon.

Outside the straw huts, the women of the village are making good use of the final hours of light: they are sorting lentils and getting the cotton ready for weaving. The shepherds are coming back from a day of work with their cows, sheep, and goats. And in the middle of the village, children are playing catch, their laughter intermingling with the calls of the cattle. From the women's house (a special building where women go to rest after birth) come the cries of babies and the calm voices of mothers.

In a few moments, the family will gather for dinner, and then my grandmother will tell a story about Jerusalem, about good and evil, about our hopes and dreams, or about whatever else is relevant. This moment is part of me, forever in my heart; here I feel most I belong. This is when and where I really felt at home!!

In 1984, when I was a little over five years old, I joined my family on the journey from Ethiopia via Sudan to the Holy Land, the land of our forefathers, the same land we were told about again and again when the family gathered after dinner. Overcoming the challenges of hunger, thirst, bandit attacks, and mental and spiritual difficulties, we made it to Israel, and since that very day, I have been looking for my time and place, that feeling of belonging, wholly, to myself and my surroundings.

As a new immigrant, I was challenged in multiple ways: language, mentality, landscape, color. We found ourselves in a new space that was preoccupied with absorbing us, and the way it chose to see us was through our "nots": What does this community *not* have? After nearly three decades of being seen this way, we had almost begun to believe that we did not have anything to give to ourselves or to society, and this was a harsh and unhealthy way of thinking.

About ten years ago, we decided we had had enough. Enough waiting for reality to change. It was time to create our own reality and our own belonging, for ourselves and our children! We decided to focus on the "haves": after all, something this community *did* possess had preserved it for twenty-five hundred years without technology or any external help from the state, back in Ethiopia.

Therefore, we invited our grandfathers and grandmothers to a plot of land, in which each participant got a share. We installed an irrigation system, and sixty-eight farmers have since been working their lots, teaching workshops on organic cultivation with the Ethiopian method and building traditional beehives. We joined the women in opening a hospitality enterprise, bringing their knowledge and skills to the forefront for them, their families, and all of Israel. Because they do have a lot to contribute!

And today, it is twilight, and the sun is reddening and setting on the horizon. From afar, among the plots of land, the black heads of elderly farmers can be seen bobbing about. As I approach with my children, a head with glad eyes pops up between the crops and invites us to pick some corn for ourselves. The children happily run to him, and the rustling of the corn in the wind mixes with their voices and those of the farmers.

In an hour or so, we will sit together in the garden, roasting the corn on the fire and listening to another Ethiopian story told by the farmers. I am home!

In our community garden in Gedera, I meet the farmers who carry inside them a breadth of time and space. They know so much and speak so little (it turns out that there are ways for deep communication other than words). They answer every "why" with "because." In them lives the clear and settled wisdom of thousands of generations. I am thrilled to discover my own strengths through them and my serenity with them, and I am delighted that this allows me, my friends, and my children to enjoy a confidence in ourselves and our surroundings.

Kalman Samuels is the founder and President of Shalva, the Israel Association for the Care and Inclusion of Persons with Disabilities. His memoir, Dreams Never Dreamed, has been published in Hebrew, English, and Japanese.

Kalman Samuels

The Shalva National Center: A Global Model of Inclusion

The Shalva National Center is a true testament to realizing our highest potential in caring for others and creating an inclusive world for all. Built in 2016, it is one of the largest and most advanced centers for inclusion and disability care in Israel, changing the standard of disability services and impacting the lives of people with disabilities in Israel and around the world.

The 220,000-square-foot structure stands tall against the breathtaking Jerusalem skyline as a welcoming beacon of hope and possibility.

Even before approaching this impressive monument of inclusion, you can witness Shalva's dedication to its mission. From the fully accessible parking lot to the inclusive community playground – Jerusalem's first public playground with fully accessible equipment – this is a place where all are welcomed and accepted.

Art is a powerful way to elevate one's surroundings and express lofty feelings and ideas that are beyond verbal expression. Shalva's use of art for its highest purpose exudes a feeling of hope, inspiration, and belonging – not only for the tens of thousands of people who rely on Shalva, but also for the many guests who come to witness this unique experience.

The *I Love You* sculpture by accomplished Israeli sculptor Sam Philipe that welcomes each visitor and participant is a constant reminder of Shalva's dedication to serving the community with love.

Right in front of the entrance to the Shalva Center is renowned Israeli artist Menashe Kadishman's iconic *Divine Utterances* sculpture. Bursting with dynamic colors and patterns, its figures resemble the form of Shalva's logo; each represents one of the ten divine utterances cited in the biblical story of Creation. This sculpture conveys that every person is a beautiful and important part of the global community.

The breathtaking three-story atrium features the vibrant and hopeful butterfly installation by award-winning Israeli artist David Gerstein, intended to uplift and welcome all who come to Shalva. Butterflies are an important motif found throughout the building and are symbolic of Shalva's children. Like caterpillars in a cocoon, their early life is challenged with limitations until they discover their wings and learn to fly – and then, the sky is the limit.

Visitors can book a comprehensive tour in advance of their visit to Shalva and experience firsthand the daily magic taking place throughout this transformative center that provides every service for people with disabilities from birth to adulthood. The Shalva Institute also offers certification courses, conferences, lectures, and workshops for disability professionals and members of the broader community who are interested in developing and enriching their understanding of disability care and inclusion.

Everything in the Shalva Center is accessible for all levels of abilities. Throughout the building, one cannot help but notice the bright colors, the uplifting murals, and even the unique pink floor tiles – everything is purposefully designed to help improve the lives of the people who come to Shalva.

Guests of the Shalva Café enjoy a deliciously inclusive experience. The café is a high-end culinary establishment and is an inclusive workplace setting which employs adults with disabilities in Shalva's employment program. The café's menu features a selection of delectable Mediterranean dishes, from hearty Israeli breakfasts to satisfying pasta meals and mouthwatering desserts. There's a reason this café is a success in its own right.

The Shalva Shop is another example of inclusion at work. It offers unique pieces including jewelry, skincare products, and more, prepared with love by our participants. Shalva is truly fulfilling the promise of creating a better and more inclusive world through all of the five senses. But as Helen Keller famously said, "The best and most beautiful things in the world cannot be seen or even touched – they must be felt with the heart."

And this is the magic hidden within Shalva. Come and feel it for yourself.

Photos courtesy of Shalva except as noted

Irina Nevzlin

Together at ANU – Museum of the Jewish People

Irina Nevzlin is an Israeli entrepreneur and author of The Impact of Identity: The Power of Knowing Who You Are. *She has served as the chair of the Board of Directors of ANU – Museum of the Jewish People since 2012.*

Growing up, I was always searching for my identity and seeking a strong sense of belonging. Whether I was aware of the complexities or not, it wasn't until I visited Israel for the first time at the age of thirteen that I felt an emotional connection to the land and its people and knew Israel was home for me.

In 2006, I immigrated to Israel and began to navigate my way around this challenging yet fulfilling new land. My father had founded the Nadav Foundation a few years prior in order to support initiatives that advance and build a substantive and pluralistic Jewish collective identity. One of these initiatives has been to support ANU – Museum of the Jewish People, as its work is the very essence of what the Nadav Foundation seeks to do in Israel and all over the world. During the same time that I was building my life in Israel, I attended a meeting for ANU, where someone hypothesized that if the museum told not only the story of the Jewish people's past, but also of its present, then it would truly fulfill its mission. This spoke to me profoundly. I truly believe that every nation deserves a place that tells its story and makes its people proud of who they are and their heritage. So, for me, the rest was history. I've been with the museum for over thirteen years now, and it is my mission and a labor of love.

ANU is the world's largest Jewish museum and the only institution that tells the unique, ongoing story of the Jewish people in its entirety, through the lens of identity, culture, and history, as well as the foundations of Jewish life and thought across generations. Most significantly, ANU is a true celebration of Jewishness, telling the story of the Jewish people through the vibrant, far-reaching rays of hope that have guided the way until today.

From the permanent exhibition at ANU
Right: facade of the eastern building, exhibits

Photos: Roni Cnaani

Photo: Yotam Ronen

Photos: Roni Cnaani

Founded in 1978 and located in Tel Aviv, the museum has recently been expanded and reimagined after a decade-long process that tripled its gallery space to 72,000 square feet (6,690 sq m), featuring four wings spanning three floors.

Adding ANU (Hebrew for "we" or "us") to the museum's name signals an embrace of broader inclusion and representation, bringing people of all backgrounds together as one. Its centerpiece is a comprehensive core exhibition that features historic and modern artifacts, images, specially produced films, multimedia displays, state-of-the-art multisensory stations and immersive spaces, as well as original and newly commissioned artworks that illuminate the more than four thousand years of the Jewish people's history in a fresh, contemporary context.

Visitors can discover awe-inspiring artifacts such as a Shaddai amulet recovered from inside the wall of an Italian home after World War II, a fifteenth-century Sephardic Book of Esther scroll, and Joseph Bentolila's letter of rights issued by Napoleon III. More contemporary beloved items include the guitar Leonard Cohen played in his final concert in Israel in 2009, pro baseball catcher turned World War II spy Moe Berg's game-worn chest protector, and Nobel Prize–winning Yiddish writer Isaac Bashevis Singer's personal typewriter.

Visitors can create their very own songs mixing tracks by Jewish musicians in all genres and use VR headsets on a musical journey of lullabies from various Jewish cultures across the centuries.

Additionally, in partnership with geni.com, the museum has developed a customized app that enables users to see if and how they're related to any famous Jew in history, and if these icons are part of the exhibition, visitors can find their location in the galleries to learn more about them. Visitors can even discover if they're related to any other person in the museum in real time, creating an immediate personal connection.

Anyone can walk into this museum and feel the pure significance of connection in just a few degrees of separation. Upholding our commitment to creating a home for all visitors to feel and experience the parallels, the relevance, and the interconnectedness of the Jewish people and this global distinction is my life's work. The museum celebrates personal identity, experiential storytelling, and innovation – a triad of Israel's most pertinent resources.

In these times of deep upheaval and renewal, seeking our truest selves and understanding our individual story has become all the more meaningful and urgent. I invite anyone and everyone to witness this magic of discovery firsthand.

Sivan Rahav-Meir

Ben Gurion Airport: Portal to the Homeland

Sivan Rahav-Meir *is a TV and radio anchor. She was chosen by* Globes *magazine as the most popular female media personality in Israel, and the* Jerusalem Post *ranked her among the fifty most influential Jewish people in the world. Sivan lectures in Israel and abroad. Her "Daily Portion" column is distributed globally.*

Why is it that to me, one of the most exciting places in Israel is this portal of entry and exit? What is so special and historic about Ben Gurion Airport?

Ever since Abraham was given the command "*lech lecha*" (go forth), Jews have been coming to Eretz Yisrael. For many years, this was no easy task. The gates to Israel were locked, and the Ottoman and British Empires placed severe limits on aliyah. Jews were being murdered in Auschwitz, but still the gates were kept closed under the British White Paper. The fact that today these gates are open, always and to everyone, is not to be taken lightly. Over the years, millions of immigrants have arrived in Israel through this, the first Israeli airport. This is where they took their first steps into their new homeland. Operation On Wings of Eagles (or "Magic Carpet"), which brought the Yemenite Jewish community to Israel in 1949–1950, arrived here, as did Operation Ezra and Nehemiah for the Jews of Iraq in 1951–1952 – and the list goes on.

Not only is this the port of entry for Diaspora Jewry, it also serves all those who love what we are building here together and who wish to visit. In 2019, over twenty-four million travelers passed through Ben Gurion Airport – whether for business, tourism, the military, work, or academia – into a country that has only nine million citizens. Twenty-four million good reasons to come here. Just recently, flights began from here to the United Arab Emirates and to Morocco, the most recent additions to the list of countries that are making peace with us.

The name of this site is also special. In July 1948, as part of Operation Dani for securing Lod and Ramle, the IDF liberated this area, where a British airport was in operation. Israel's first prime minister, David Ben-Gurion, wrote in his diary: "The tremendous accomplishments in the few days following the truce are almost inconceivable. The airport is in our hands – who knows whether the Israeli government would have built such an airport in a decade. It

Photo: Chris Hoare (CC BY 2.0)

Photo: Davidi Vardi Pikiwiki Israel (CC BY 2.5)

is almost complete." He certainly never imagined how this airport would grow – and that it would be named after him.

The human mix at the airport is always varied, and for some reason – perhaps because they're all waiting for a flight – there are no conflicts between Jews and Arabs, religious and secular, locals and foreigners. Perhaps the proximity to the heavens leads many to stop at the Chabad House at the airport, to lay tefillin and give charity before their flight. A plane taking off from Ben Gurion is one of the only places where ultra-Orthodox and secular, Israeli and tourist can have long, meaningful conversations.

I always resolve to arrive early for my flights, so that I can see the rotating photography display in the long hallway that leads to the flight gates. One side of this 180-meter-long hall is paneled in Jerusalem stone, while on the other, daylight streams through a vast picture window. Fascinating photographs are displayed on one wall: Israel's Independence Day, important moments from the Knesset – an attempt to capture the spirit of Israeli society. But somehow, in the end I always find myself running to my flight.

There've been so many of these beautiful exhibitions that I haven't had time to stop and see.

During the lockdowns in the era of COVID-19, it was practically impossible to get into the country. During this period, I held endless conversations over Zoom with communities abroad, and each time I heard how much they missed it and how hard it was for them that Israel's gates were suddenly closed. "I used to think I could always buy a flight ticket – that I was just one flight ticket away from my homeland," one woman told me at a lecture to the Baltimore community. "But now Ben Gurion Airport is closed."

Once again, Jews could not fulfill the command of *lech lecha* and go to Israel – although the circumstances were new. During a Zoom lecture to the Panama community, one of the participants asked me to open the window behind me so she could catch a glimpse of Jerusalem. I opened the window in my office. Behind me, all she could see were a few dark buildings – but this sight was enough to bring tears of emotion to her eyes.

PART IV

SPIRITUALITY
History of the Jewish People

Rabbi Shmuel Rabinovitch

The Western Wall in the Holy City of Jerusalem

Rabbi Shmuel Rabinovitch *is Rabbi of the Western Wall and the Holy Sites. A graduate of Yeshivat Kol Torah in Jerusalem, he served in the IDF in the military rabbinate. He has published several books on Jewish law and Scripture.*

Ever since I was appointed Rabbi of the Western Wall, I make my way every morning to the Kotel (Western Wall) in Jerusalem as if for the first time. Nowhere else in the entire world do I feel so connected. What is the secret behind this ancient, lofty wall of stones, which carries so much emotional and spiritual weight?

After the Second Temple was destroyed by the Roman Legion in 70 CE, the Jewish people were forbidden from praying on the holy Temple Mount (due to halachic constraints and later to Muslim objections). Instead, they went to pray at the foot of the western wall of the Temple Mount, the wall closest to the Foundation Stone – the holiest point on the mountain and the site of the Holy of Holies, the heart of the Temple. Throughout the long years of the exile and to this day, Jews have carried the memory of the Kotel in their hearts, and its image became the symbol of the longing for Zion. We pray to experience "next year in the rebuilt Jerusalem."

Naturally, then, when the Jewish people began to return to the Land of Israel, they first went to Jerusalem. In 1267, when Rabbi Moses ben Nachman (the Ramban) made the dangerous journey from Spain to Jerusalem to renew the Jewish settlement there, Jerusalem was in ruins, poor and tarnished. But it was his city. The only city in the world where the Temple had stood. The only city in the world that was his home, the home that belonged to all of us.

Through the millennia, while Jerusalem passed through the hands of a long list of rulers, generations of pilgrims came to pour out their hearts in prayer before the ancient stones. In the narrow alley where the Muslim and British authorities permitted prayer, Jews gathered

from all four corners of the earth, vowing repeatedly, "If I forget you, O Jerusalem, may my right hand forget its cunning" (Psalms 137:5).

After the declaration of the establishment of the State of Israel, the Jordanian army invaded and occupied the Old City of Jerusalem. They expelled the Jewish residents of the Old City, including my late grandfather, Rabbi Shmuel Benzion Rabinovitch, whose name I bear, and his son, my father. Immediately after the battles ended, the ceasefire agreements were violated, and Jews were completely forbidden from entering the Old City and visiting the Kotel. For nineteen years, no Jewish hand touched its stones. Then during the Six-Day War, IDF forces liberated the Kotel from its occupiers. "I felt as if I was standing there," said one soldier, "and all of Jewish history was standing there with me."

After the war, tens of thousands of Jews rushed to the Western Wall Plaza. Many of them had been born after the Jordanian occupation of the Old City and had never seen the Kotel. Today the Kotel has become the most visited site in the State of Israel. It is also a premier historical and archeological site, containing findings from the beginning of Jewish settlement in Jerusalem three thousand years ago and continuing through all the periods of Jerusalem's past.

Our Sages relate in the Babylonian Talmud (*Makkot* 24b) that Rabbi Akiva, when touring the ruins of the Temple, laughed upon seeing a fox running out from the place of the Holy of Holies. His companions, weeping at the degradation of the site, asked him how he could possibly laugh. He told them that the prophets wrote about the destruction of Jerusalem (Micah 3:12,

Photos: Western Wall Heritage Foundation

Jeremiah 26:18–20) and also about its redemption (Zechariah 8:4). Seeing that the first prophecy had come true gave him certain knowledge that the second would as well, and thus he laughed in joy. And his companions were comforted.

So many generations have passed since Rabbi Akiva comforted his companions before the ruins of Jerusalem. And with our own eyes, the members of my generation have seen the words of the prophet Zechariah (8:4–5), "There shall yet old men and old women sit in the broad places of Jerusalem … And the broad places of the city shall be full of boys and girls playing in the broad places thereof." At the center of this prophecy is the great plaza of the Kotel, the remnant of the Temple. Each year, over twelve million visitors and worshippers visit this holy site, which not so long ago was a tiny, isolated alley, a symbol of the Jewish people's humiliation at the hands of other nations.

As part of my complex position as Rabbi of the Western Wall, each day I stand before the window of my office and look out at the people in the plaza – the bar mitzvah boys celebrating with their families, Torah scrolls in their arms; young girls watching with fascination as an elderly woman recites Psalms; soldiers dancing with yeshiva students, their heads covered with berets in all colors of the rainbow. I see them approaching the Kotel like ships returning to their home ports, seeking to meet the one thing that no other place in the world can offer them – their heritage and their past.

Here at the Western Wall, they experience a sanctity that draws its strength from centuries of longing and prayer. Through this power, the Kotel ignites the soul.

Dr. Yael Gold-Zamir is a mother, medical doctor, and entrepreneur. She founded Embryonics, an AI company that applies deep learning to improve success rates of fertility treatments, and Gold Health, a global medical intelligence and expert relations firm. She holds an MD from the Hebrew University of Jerusalem.

Dr. Yael Gold-Zamir

Praying for Clarity Together at the Kotel

There's a small segment of an ancient retaining wall in Jerusalem built of massive limestone blocks with finely chiseled borders. It is the heart of the Old City of Jerusalem and it has, for millennia, been a symbol of faith, of holiness, and of hope. Of course, it is the Kotel Hamaaravi, the Western Wall, which is literally the western retaining wall of the Temple Mount, the ancient site of the First and Second Jewish Temples. For me, there is simply no other place that so represents Israel.

The Kotel is not inherently holy; rather, its holiness comes from its proximity to the Temple Mount, and, specifically, the Holy of Holies, the inner sanctuary of the Holy Temple when it stood nearly two thousand years ago. It's that proximity that has transformed the site into a magnet of splendor and hope for millions of people every year.

I am one of those people. Every significant step or moment in my life has been coupled by a visit to the Kotel – and there have been some pretty significant moments.

As a Jewish woman from the ultra-Orthodox community, I've taken a rather unorthodox path. The traditional schooling system in our community calls for separate education for girls and boys, and university is discouraged. Higher education often takes the form of a degree program, often run by ultra-Orthodox institutions, with a faster track to a profession while remaining in the protected environment of the community. But my chosen profession took me on a new and unusual path.

About fifteen years ago, I was the first in my community to apply – and get accepted to – medical school. Then, I became the first doctor in the community, blazing a trail for dozens of ultra-Orthodox medical students after me. As a medical doctor fascinated by the science behind fertility, I led a big research project that turned into a successful company called Embryonics that develops cutting-edge technology to improve the process and results of fertility treatments. For me, it was a convergence of Israel and my Jewish identity together with innovation and science.

Photo: Pinchas Shtern (CC BY 2.5)

These were enormous steps to take. Each decision, every part of the process, involved taking a trip to the Kotel to pour my heart out in prayer to make the best decision and receive God's blessing.

The Kotel is truly for everyone, of any religion, age, social status – in fact, even this is part of its story. Legend tells that the western retaining wall was built by the poor people. It wasn't about gold or opulence, about honor or status; rather, it was a wall that was built by and accessible to all.

Since 1967, in the aftermath of the Six-Day War, everyone – Jew and non-Jew, and every person from all over the world – can access the Kotel in its expanded public square. People can pray, think, meditate, or experience it in any way of their choosing, whether deeply personal (such as placing a note to God in the cracks of the ancient stones), public (such as IDF induction ceremonies), or ceremonial (such as bar or bat mitzvah celebrations).

I have always felt an incredible pull to the Kotel. I go whenever I have time and stand close to its ancient stones, praying for clarity in some important decision. Or I stand at the back, where I can see

Photo: Moses Pini Siluk

the whole wall at once, and observe all the people there – people of every type, from all over the world, speaking every language, all making the deliberate choice, at that moment, to find themselves at that holy place.

Any time you find your way to the Kotel, you are unlikely to be alone. Even a snowstorm or a driving rain won't keep people away. The place is so inspiring to everyone, and seeing how everyone finds his or her own unique connection to the place is further inspiring.

As I traverse those seemingly magical alleys of the Old City, I can feel the rich history that permeates every rock; I can smell those authentic aromas coming from eateries representing the tapestry of cultures and religions; I can hear the noises coming from the multitude of yeshivot as well as soldiers, tourists from all over the world, and so many people all going in one particular direction… So just follow the current and you will get there… This is my Israel.

Rabbi Binyamin Lau

The Outlook from Ma'alot Benny ("Benny's Ascent")

Rabbi Binyamin Lau *is the head of the 929: Tanach B'yakhad educational project and former head of the Human Rights and Judaism in Action Project at the Israel Democracy Institute. He served as spiritual leader of the Ramban Synagogue in Jerusalem for eighteen years. He lives in Jerusalem.*

Ma'alot Benny, named after Benny Marshak, a cofounder of the IDF Education Corps, is a pedestrian path that leads from West Jerusalem through the Valley of Hinnom (Gey Ben Hinnom) up to Mount Zion and into the Old City. This ascent, accessible from all directions, is a point of connection between East and West, past and future, sacred and profane, heaven and earth.

At the bottom of the ascent, Hebron Road guides our gaze along the north-south axis – from Megiddo in the north to Be'er Sheva in the south. Throughout human history, pedestrians traveling from the northern empires to the southern kingdom of Egypt had to follow this route. Jaffa Road directs our view along the east-west axis. At its far western point lies Jaffa, the ancient maritime gateway to the Land of Israel. Walking east along this road leads to the Old City and the sacred space of the world's three major monotheistic religions.

Ma'alot Benny borders the deep gorge of the Valley of Hinnom. Today, the Jerusalem Cinematheque enhances the edge of the valley, but history commemorates this as the site of human sacrifice to the gods in the cult of Molech. On a clear day, the view from this valley to the eastern horizon stretches all the way to the Dead Sea.

This path invites entry to another dimension in time and space. Walking along the leafy path, you wind from south to north and west to east, then north to south and again to the east, until you reach the ascent to Mount Zion, where you encounter the walls of the Old City and the Zion Gate entrance.

My first steps up the path lead north, but my gaze is drawn to the magnificent view in the west, where open terrain extends to the horizon. The hilly landscape is dotted with neighborhoods. The closest is Yemin Moshe, recognizable by its famous windmill. Next to it is Mishkenot Sha'ananim, constructed by Moses Montefiore to encourage Jerusalem's poor to leave the constricted walls of the Old City. In the 1860s, these neighborhoods marked the beginning of a fresh movement within Judaism – free from confinement inside the walls, it heralded the choice of a new life. How brave were those first Jews who dared to break through the walls and venture out into the open spaces.

As the path turns, my eye moves east and meets the bell tower atop King David's tomb on Mount Zion. This site is the birthplace of the powerful narrative that binds the three monotheistic religions at one momentous point – David's choice of Jerusalem as the capital of Israel. This site on Mount Zion and eastward (Mount Moriah) had belonged to the Jebusites. During Joshua's period of leadership, the Jebusites occupied an enclave set among the Israelite tribes, between Benjamin to the north and Judah to the south. David took over the Jebusite enclave and made it his universal capital, belonging to all the tribes. Jerusalem was first built by a human king who recognized the dominion of the universal King of kings.

As I walk, my thoughts roam to the charm of this city. Jerusalem is meant to be a place of reconciliation, connecting a unified community of believers, but over the centuries of history of the monotheistic religions, it has tragically become a city of strife and conflict.

Still deep in thought, I arrive at the entrance to Zion Gate. This is the main entrance into the Old City, and from it, the road leads downward to the Western Wall and Mount Moriah. For thousands of years, the Western Wall was the focus of Jewish longing for generations of Jewish dreamers who envisioned Jerusalem as the beating heart of their people. During the War of Independence, the Old City was cut off, and West and East Jerusalem were divided by a border. The Six-Day War reunited the city, and now we barely take notice when we pass between the two sides.

I stop at this now imaginary border and give thanks to the generations that preceded me – the generations of Jews who dreamed but did not live to see it, and the generation that dreamed and witnessed the dream come true. My generation bears the responsibility for preserving this dream and for fostering the next stage of its realization – to transform Jerusalem into a city of peace, one that includes all its dreamers, a place that acts as a connecting point between East and West, past and future, sacred and profane, heaven and earth.

View from the amphitheater at Mount Scopus (photo: Dr. Avishai Teicher Pikiwiki Israel [CC BY 2.5])

Rabbi Mordechai Bar-Or

Life and Abyss at the Foundation Stone, Temple Mount

As a child in the Ramat Eshkol neighborhood of Jerusalem, I would walk every Friday evening alone through Nablus Gate to the Western Wall. I would lean against the enormous stones and place my head against the hundreds of personal notes that people had written from the depths of their hearts, and chant the Song of Songs in the traditional melody. Undoubtedly, there was something mysterious about the Temple Mount that drew me to walk all that way from my parents' home.

Jerusalem is one of the most emotionally charged cities in the world. Some visit it with joy, others with hesitation or out of a sense of duty. But all agree that this city contains unique energy and great mystery.

The Western Wall surrounds the Even Hashtiyah (Foundation Stone), which was inside the Temple. What does the Foundation Stone conceal?

The Midrash says (*Tanchuma*, Kedoshim 10):

> Just as a navel is set in the middle of a person, so the Land of Israel is the navel of the world. Thus it is stated (in Ezek. 38:12), "who dwell on the navel of the earth." ...The Land of Israel sits at the center of the world; Jerusalem is in the center of the Land of Israel; the Sanctuary is in the center of Jerusalem; the Temple building is in the center of the Sanctuary; the Holy Ark is in the center of the Temple building; and the Foundation Stone, out of which the world was founded, is in front of the Temple building.

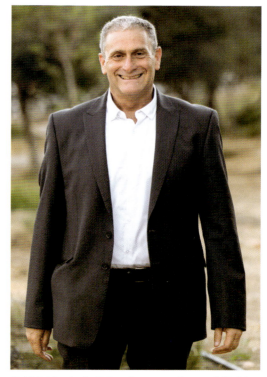

Rabbi Mordechai Bar-Or, *a graduate of Yeshivat Har Etzion, was the founder and director of the Jewish leadership training institute Kolot. He is currently leading the initiative V'heye B'racha on the vision of the Jewish people in this era. His book on this theme came out in late 2022.*

According to many midrashic sources, the Foundation Stone is the place where God sealed the abyss that remained from the beginning of Creation (see *Targum Yerushalmi*, Exodus 28:30: "[God's Holy Name was] engraved and expressed in the Foundation Stone, with which the Master of the world sealed up the mouth of the great deep at the beginning"). God sealed the abyss underneath the Foundation Stone to enable the world to exist. He did not erase it, but only buried it for the future of humanity.

If the stone is touched in the wrong way, the entire world may be washed away like in the biblical flood. This is why the Temple Mount is such a sensitive place.

The Foundation Stone is not only the place where the Creation began. It is also the source of the world's enduring vitality. The tendons and capillaries that extend from it nourish the entire world with vitality and abundance. The Foundation Stone thus contains a duality of extremes – on the one hand, the world's vitality and life force flows from it; on the other, it contains the essence of chaos and nothingness.

With the Foundation Stone at its center, Jerusalem is an invitation to the world to overcome this duality – to observe the foundations of Creation and the abyss within ourselves and thus to touch the meaning of existence. After being banished from Eden, humanity longs for the fundamental instincts that operated there. Humanity has an inner desire for a renewed encounter with the infinite, in the physical dimension on Earth.

Jerusalem demands a different kind of conversation. As the abyss is part of its very character and location, the usual Western-style dialogue cannot succeed here in this city. In Jerusalem, a solution based on a Western ethical dialogue of good and bad cannot work. The linguistic categories of "occupation" and "liberation" that are part of ordinary consciousness limit its significance. They do not touch the hidden secret embodied by this city.

Jerusalem demands exploration and inquiry. It requires that we touch its vital core, its power, and its potential for life, in a balanced, peaceful manner.

Original Study finished on the Spot by Carl Haag, June 1859

Jerusalem is a city of *tohu va'vohu* – "formless and void" (Genesis 1:2). At any moment, the abyss may open up, releasing a flood that will sweep away the Land of Israel or even the entire world. The conversation on Jerusalem must touch the connection between the forces of chaos and the powerful prayer for peace shared by all existence.

A new conversation on Jerusalem has the power to transform this city into far more than the capital of Israel – it can become the heart of the entire world, a "house of prayer for all peoples" (Isaiah 56:7), "and in you, all the families of the earth will be blessed" (Genesis 12:3).

Lior Suchard

The Binding of Isaac: A True Story, or Not

On the eastern border of Jerusalem's Old City, between the Jewish and the Muslim Quarters, sits a walled compound of approximately thirty-five acres, over which nations have fought and dreamt for hundreds of generations. One mountain, three nations worshipping it, and a long history soaked with blood, miracles, and wonders.

Just one glance toward the gilded dome of the Al Aqsa Mosque brings up the entirety of the history bubbling under the surface, and I am swept back in time to an astonishing story to which I keep coming back. You probably know the story very well: in it, Abraham went up Mount Moriah to sacrifice his only son Isaac, facing one of the hardest trials a man can suffer. I stand on the balcony, imagining a deep, hidden voice calling with authority, "Lay not thine hand upon the lad …"

I am suddenly struck with a curious, intriguing thought: What if Abraham did not meet an angel there, on Mount Moriah? What if it was his *yiddishe kop* (Jewish wisdom) helping him find such a good cover story that anyone hearing it was convinced?

Let us ride our time machine four thousand years back. In that time, a custom was prevalent among the inhabitants of Canaan to sacrifice children to the god Ba'al. According to the Canaanite faith, such a sacrifice would ensure wealth, health, and fruitfulness and cause the god to forget his wrath. Archeological evidence found in the Valley of Hinnom supports this. Abraham returns from Mesopotamia and is exposed to the customs of the local idolators. He understands he must act like them and obey the laws of the king and is therefore to sacrifice his son. He has no options.

Lior Suchard *is a master mentalist and entrepreneur. Considered to be the best in the world, he has performed in over sixty countries and is one of the most in-demand performers among Fortune 500 companies. Lior has appeared on Jay Leno, Larry King, James Corden, and numerous other shows.*

He is standing there, on that mountain, with Isaac next to him and the knife in his hand, and unimaginable things are happening inside him, as it looks as if he is not going to be able to escape this wretched business. He is telling himself (and rightly so), "I should kill my son? Am I insane?" But the order is an order, everyone is expecting a sacrifice, and he must provide it lest he himself become a burnt offering together with his whole family.

And then the idea hits him! A spark of creativity, daring, and, yes, chutzpah! "Come, we are leaving!" says Abraham as he hurries down the mountain with his son at his heels. Abraham is excited and thrilled – he is about to put on a show!

Four thousand years later his descendants will be the ones winning more Nobel prizes than any nation, turning two millennia of survival into a "start-up nation" in what in historical terms is no time at all. Who gave us, the Jewish people, the genes of creativity if not the father of our nation?

"Don't ask what happened," he tells the locals, shaking all over.

"What happened?" they immediately demand.

And because they ask, he tells them. He summons all of his storytelling abilities and tells them a story that has never been told before and that will, with time, turn into a best seller. He knows that Isaac's life depends on it. "I met an angel. A real-life angel, with wings and all, and it told me not to touch the kid. It had a deep voice, and it said *lay not thine hand upon the lad, neither do thou any thing unto him*."

"But what about the sacrifice?" they asked.

"The angel then showed me a ram, and I brought the ram as a sacrifice instead. God is happy, my friends."

Animal sacrifice instead of human sacrifice is born as a concept.

The Canaanites are shocked. None of them have ever met an angel, especially not one that could fly and talk. Abraham amazes and fascinates them with his story while reshaping their minds. Like a great mentalist, a seasoned performer, he manages to affect their thinking and employ suggestion. He has the crowd in his thrall. The locals believe that such is the will of the gods. When the performance is creative enough and the magic feels real, all that is left for the audience to say is "Wow!" And the rest is history.

In my shows, I cause amazement, creating the impossible on a daily basis and playing with people's minds. Maybe Abraham was like that as well. Maybe he, too, was a sort of mentalist, even if he ended up there against his will. Whether Abraham fabricated the binding story or actually experienced it as told in the Book of Genesis, it is a defining moment in the DNA of the Jewish people.

My story may not be true at all, but what if we allowed ourselves to let go of the story and accept the miracle? What if we told ourselves a new story that would permit us to create a new reality, in which the Temple Mount is open to everyone, and there is no more conflict, and our story intertwines in harmony with that of our neighbors, and we do not need to make any more sacrifices?

The Temple Mount – Lior Suchard 133

Sharonna Karni Cohen is an artivist and entrepreneur. She is the CEO and cocreator at Dreame, a platform for cocreating art with hundreds of artists around the world, and the creator of the Big Dream installation, traveling globally and in space, envisioning the future of the world.

Sharonna Karni Cohen

Dreaming at the Austrian Hospice

The Austrian Hospice does not have its doors open awaiting your arrival. On the contrary. You ring a small and almost secret doorbell, and, open sesame, the gates unbolt. Upon entering, you are met with a beautiful staircase, echoing with history and spirituality.

I was first taken here by a friend. He knew every place in Israel and how to navigate through life, but it's easy to lose your sense of direction as you walk among the stalls in the Jerusalem markets. Sometimes you turn left and end up somewhere completely different from where you thought you were going.

As we walked, neither he nor I knowing exactly where we were headed, we found ourselves entering the Via Dolorosa. He became excited, remembering a place he'd like to show me.

For me, this is Israel. Uncertainty, adventure, journeys, a sense of home, and magic all around you. Getting lost and being spontaneous is part of the game, as long as you always believe you'll reach your destination in the end.

I began my career as an entrepreneur after meeting two tech founders on a bench in Tel Aviv. We sat for hours chatting. Their company, WSC, creates sports highlights. They inspired me and became my good friends. I seek mystery alongside meaning and believe that in Israel it's easy to spot the signs everywhere you go and with everyone you meet, since it's such a small country but with so much depth.

I've had my fair share of challenges since starting my own company, Dreame, an online and offline experience for commissioning custom-made artworks from a collective of artists around the world. I am inspired by the equally spontaneous and rational minds here in Israel and believe this to be the cause of my resilience. I also believe in never giving up, no matter how hard it may get.

Via Dolorosa means "Path of Sorrow" in Latin: it is believed to be the road Jesus took on the way to his crucifixion. On one side of it sprawls the Arab Market, on the other the Jewish, and in between are many churches. Walking along the winding path, one is reminded of the layers of religious observance in Jerusalem.

The Austrian Hospice's roof terrace café affords a panoramic view of Jerusalem as well as a dazzling soundscape. The Austrian Hospice is the oldest Christian guesthouse in the Holy City. It often hosts exhibitions and events dedicated to cultural inclusion, as well as discussions of local, national, and international social issues.

I recommend having the apple strudel with an iced coffee. I also suggest bringing a journal, and, even if visiting with friends, taking a moment to reflect on your own past, present, and future. Note the hardships that have made you stronger, write down the signs that help your intuition answer your persistent questions, and make a list of dreams for the year ahead.

Photo: courtesy of the Austrian Hospice

Tamara Kolitz, MD, is Founder and Chairperson of the nonprofit organization Lema'anam – Physicians for Holocaust Survivors. She is a graduate of the Sackler Faculty of Medicine at Tel Aviv University, an internal medicine specialist and an endocrinology fellow at the Tel Aviv Sourasky Medical Center. She is a mother of two and lives in Tel Aviv.

Tamara Kolitz

The Forest of the Martyrs, Where Every Person Has a Tree

Ten years ago, in a small souvenir shop on the edge of Budapest's Jewish cemetery, my father discovered a prayer shawl crown. When he returned to Israel, he had the ornate embroidered silver ornament sewn onto his prayer shawl.

"Every time I wrap myself in my prayer shawl," he told me recently, "I wonder whose crown it was. Who was that man? What was he dreaming of? What became of him? Perhaps he survived and is still alive? What was his name?"

When my father told me this, I thought of Zelda's poem "Each of Us Has a Name."

It was in my parents' home that I discovered how Hebrew poetry is bound up with our past and with places in Israel. Classic Israeli songs formed the soundtrack of my childhood. My Sabbath memories were made of the words and melodies that I inhabited as I sailed through their spaces.

My father grew up in a religious home, and we too observed the Sabbath. Like my classmates, every Sunday I would come to school filled with my Sabbath travel adventures from all the places I had visited – in my imagination. Of all the places I have visited, whether on the wings of my imagination or in real life, my heart belongs to the Forest of the Martyrs. I discovered the forest on a high school trip, and since then, every time I go to the mountains of Jerusalem, to the forest, I hear Zelda's words.

The Forest of the Martyrs is a living monument to the victims of the Holocaust, planted with six million trees: every person has a tree. Along the banks of the Kisalon River, each section of the forest commemorates a different Jewish community destroyed in the Holocaust, and in each section, the trees number the sum of the dead. The Scroll of Fire sits in the center of the woods, a memorial in the form of two Torah scrolls: the one, ruin and destruction, the other revival and independence.

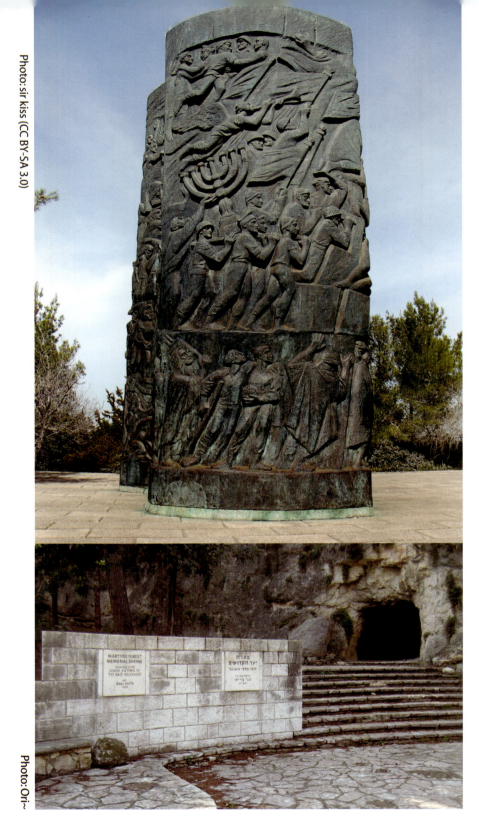

From there, the path winds its way down to the Anne Frank memorial, where a steel frame evokes a small room. Inside, a seat faces a wall through which one can see a chestnut tree, like the one Anne wrote of in her diary. The memorial recalls the routine of life in hiding and the yearning for freedom. Fragments of hope.

The forest changes colors with the seasons. In spring, wildflowers paint it pink and white, sage and cistus. In winter, anemones and cyclamens join in. Bindweed, adorned with heart-shaped leaves, forms a tangle in the trees.

I shudder every time I wander among the pines and cypresses, the oaks, the pistacias, and the eucalyptus – trees that are so characteristic of this land. I see not only six million green memorial candles, but also the natural growth of a wondrous nature which the human hand has barely shaped.

The pain and loneliness of Holocaust survivors have resonated with me all these years. As a doctor, I would occasionally discover a Holocaust identification number tattooed on a patient's forearm. This led me to establish a nonprofit association offering free medical care for Holocaust survivors – my own "private forest," if you will.

And if the trees planted in memory of those who perished can regenerate life, there is hope; we, the next generation, can nourish the roots that have given us life and try to create a world that is just a little more beautiful.

We who grew up in this country now have children of our own. "Get up and walk this land with a backpack and a walking stick," my sons sing on our way to a family hiking trip in the Judean Desert, as we leave the crowded streets of Tel Aviv behind. As the city streets turn into the yellow sands, I hear "Like a Ballad" in my mind, a song by Natan Yonatan, whose son Lior fell in the Yom Kippur War. A song of love and sacrifice to the land in which we live with the most demanding, addictive joy in the present while remembering and respecting the past, nourishing our children with the childhood experiences that will live on as they continue down their own paths.

Every Sabbath in the synagogue, when my father wraps himself in his prayer shawl, he too continues, if only a little, the life of one person who had a name and for whom the crown bears witness.

PART V

CULTURE AND LEISURE
Life in Israel

David Broza

Masada and My Sunrise Concerts

David Broza *is an internationally renowned singer-songwriter, recognized for his dynamic guitar performances and humanitarian efforts. His signature sound brings together songs in Hebrew, Spanish, and English, with the influence of Spanish flamenco, American folk, rock and roll, and poetry. He has released over forty albums, many of which are multiplatinum.*

On July 14, 1993, I was driving with my selected band of great musicians to perform what would become my Masada Sunrise Concert. I knew this was going to be a special event. It was not quite clear to me how it would be staged; I just had a gut feeling this was going to be a three-hour show, and that I should also record and film it. The night before, I had managed to recruit the recording studio and a film production company to make their way to the site. This was not a simple operation, as conditions in the desert can be treacherous, with wild gusts of wind and dust that can go on all night and make the operation of a show very difficult.

Masada is a place we know for historic martyrdom and bravery – its unique spirit symbolizes spiritual heroism to Israelis and the entire Jewish world. The magical spell of the desert, with the Dead Sea and the Jordan Valley, the harsh climate, and the open skies, is simply incredible. But upon arrival at the scene of the concert, none of this was in evidence. The stage was small, and the mobile recording studio and film crew were feverishly struggling to set up in time. No one, including myself, knew how things would unfold. I had a song list but no set list. Everyone was going to follow me as I charged forward and created the show in real time.

The event was completely sold out. The audience was mostly young people – from teenagers up to about mid-thirties. It was a moonless night, which meant that even I had no clue how the sunrise would look or even from which direction the sun would come up. I had never thought to ask. The show was starting at three in the morning. At two, as we finished the last-minute arrangements, we felt a light gust of wind. No one seemed too worried. At two thirty, it got stronger. I asked Mousa, the local Bedouin on the Masada crew, when the wind would stop. He said "soon" and laughed. Meanwhile, the crowds were pouring in and settling in their seats.

Performance photos here and right: Ra'anan Cohen

At three o'clock sharp, I got onstage and started playing. The audience was radiant and energetic, and the gusts of wind added atmosphere. I was very focused at first, but as the wind became stronger, I began looking for Mousa. I needed him to tell me if the show might be sabotaged by this. I saw him at the side of the stage enjoying the music and the scene and asked that he come up onstage and sit next to me to monitor the weather. The wind got worse and worse, but I continued performing in full force. The audience was singing loudly with me, and the band was "kicking ass," as we say in rock 'n' roll. I was in a trance-like state and totally into the performance.

At about five thirty in the morning, I started seeing the faces of the audience. A few minutes later, I looked behind me to see the band and where we were, and I was overwhelmed. It seemed as if we were up in the heavens. The Masada fortress was directly behind me, and behind it lay the Dead Sea – the lowest geographic point on the globe – with the valley in between covered in a nebulous blanket of dew. We were above the clouds. It was nature in all its glory. I kept playing and felt the feverish energy of the audience rising – all passion and love with no concern for time and place. We were all of one mind and breathing together. Heavenly.

The next time I looked back, the sun was rising in the sky, and the dew blanket was evaporating. The fortress and northern palace of Masada, built two thousand years ago by King Herod, stood behind us. The ramp that the Romans used to take over the fortress, where they found all the zealots dead... All of that beauty and history rushed through my blood. I was moving into the final shot of energy and raising the entire crowd into a climactic celebration of love and freedom and exhilaration. This was my first Masada Sunrise Show.

Since 1993, with few exceptions, I have returned to perform the Sunrise Show every year. It has become a part of my annual tour, and I shall continue to look forward to performing there until my last breath.

Shira Rivelis *is a trusted ghostwriter and writing consultant for some of Israel's leading executives, entrepreneurs, and investors. She has over a decade of experience running her own content agency. Shira holds a master's degree in English literature and language from the University of Amsterdam.*

Shira Rivelis

A Dose of Optimism at Tmol Shilshom

Situated in a picturesque alleyway of one of the first neighborhoods to be built outside the Old City of Jerusalem, Tmol Shilshom is a hidden gem thick with atmosphere.

The road to this part restaurant, part cultural institution takes visitors through the winding archways and hidden niches of the Nachalat Shiva neighborhood to 5 Yoel Moshe Salomon Street. From there, 130-year-old steps lead to a nostalgic bookstore café.

The space features wall-to-wall books, an eclectic decor of antique chairs and couches, exposed limestone arches, menus printed on the inside of old book covers, and dairy vegetarian delicacies served on china plates patterned with poetry and prose.

Founded by David Ehrlich and Dan Goldberg in 1994, Tmol Shilshom was named after a book of the same name, *Only Yesterday* by Nobel Prize laureate Shmuel Yosef (S. Y.) Agnon. In both name and ambience, it is thus profoundly tied to the world of Hebrew literature.

The many literary figures who adopted Tmol Shilshom over the past three decades – including Yehuda Amichai, Amos Oz, A. B. Yehoshua, David Grossman, Batya Gur, Orly Castel-Bloom, and others – have helped turn the café into a Jerusalem writers' haven. Today, the venue regularly hosts book launches and open mic nights for young poets, as well as lectures, conferences, workshops, and family events.

My love for the written word was born in the comfy armchair of this café. As a child, I spent many an afternoon scrooched down by the small window table, pen in hand and nursing a bowl of tomato soup.

With time, my visits grew less frequent. Months would go by before I revisited my favorite café in the city. But regardless of how much time passes, something about walking down the cool cobblestone road and breathing in the smell of old books always feels like home.

In early 2010, I joined the IDF. I was a *tazpitanit* (field observer) in charge of tracking the fence along the Gaza border. It was a complex job that required me to be someone I did not necessarily want to be. Walking around my hometown on weekend visits in my olive green *madei alef* (service uniform) felt like being in a play.

It was around that time that, together with a photographer friend of mine, I entered the open call for photography at Tmol Shilshom. The idea was for me to pose as different characters sitting around the same table. The photo shoot quickly turned into a playful afternoon of dress-up. The waiters were amused to see me go behind the folding screen with my military uniform and come out wearing a second-hand tailored vintage dress and floppy hat. One moment I was a novelist sipping a glass of wine, and the next I was a frisky teenager in a polka dot dress. For those few brief hours, I forgot about my role as an IDF soldier. I put the complex, often violent political reality of living in Jerusalem out of my mind and embodied the role my vintage costume dictated.

Looking at that winning photograph more than a decade later, I now realize that the charm of Tmol Shilshom is in its ability to encapsulate a sense of normalcy and optimism in the midst of chaos.

Like the people of Jerusalem, Tmol Shilshom has struggled to keep its head up through the Second Intifada in 2000, rocket attacks from Gaza in 2014, the personal loss of a loved one (Tmol Shilshom lost its founder and co-owner David Ehrlich following a sudden heart attack), and the worldwide lockdowns imposed due to the pandemic in 2020.

Through it all, Tmol Shilshom continues to produce art and poetry and to be a home to anyone who wishes to set aside political, religious, and cultural roles for the sake of having a quiet conversation over hot cocoa with extra whipped cream.

The winning contest photo, 2010 (photo: Smadar Tsook)

Dr. Avital Beck

The Bustle of Jerusalem's Central Bus Station

Jerusalem's Central Bus Station is the beating heart of Jerusalem, the capital city of Israel, and it's an anthropologically fascinating place to visit. For decades, the Central Bus Station was a grubby, windswept glorified parking lot with nothing but platforms for the buses and the occasional falafel stand – not exactly what you would expect in Israel's largest city.

In fact, it wasn't until September 2001 that Israel's capital finally got the transportation hub it truly deserved. Opening to great fanfare, the new station introduced a previously unknown level of convenience. For one thing, it allowed Jerusalemites to wait for their buses without having to surrender themselves to the elements. The full-blown mall that came with it was also a breath of fresh air, with the requisite cafés, shawarma stands, food court, and synagogue, as well as clothing stores, bookstores, and an assortment of other spots where one could squander a hard-earned shekel.

I find Jerusalem's Central Bus Station to be a microcosm of Israel's heterogeneity, passion, and diversity. I don't mind driving my car to the city, but whenever I travel to Jerusalem for business or shopping, I insist on taking the bus. I love the hectic atmosphere that hits me when I walk into the station. The sounds, the smells, the shops, the bustle – it all opens my mind and heart.

I also enjoy seeing how the station changes its colors to suit the huge conferences held in the Binyanei Hauma convention center across the street.

When I come to Binyan Shalem, an annual summer conference of five thousand religious

Avital Beck, **PhD**, **MBA**, *is a serial entrepreneur in the world of peak performance. She is the CEO and cofounder of GISCOPE; former CEO, CSO, and cofounder of DiagnoseStick; and cofounder of NERA to promote orthodox women in high tech. The mother of seven children, she is an expert in medical and biotech innovation.*

mothers coming to learn Torah, the whole station is full of women in colorful head scarves running to learn. The shops in the station display a profusion of targeted merchandise, offering head coverings, baby clothes, and modest women's clothing.

When it's time for business conferences, the station is turned black and white (and gray), with all the people in suits rushing to business meetings. The shop owners then put out electronic gadgets, earphones, and computer accessories.

During my medical studies in Jerusalem, the station was a symbol of home after a week of learning day and night in the dormitories of the Hebrew University of Jerusalem. It was a feeling of freedom when I was hurrying home for Shabbat.

But most of all, Jerusalem's Central Bus Station reminds me of the 2001 Intifada. I was doing my National Service in central Jerusalem, and buses were exploding around us every week. Every trip from the dorms to work felt as if it would take a miracle to stay alive. More than once, I found myself getting off a bus mid-way because someone seemed suspicious, or I had a bad feeling. Israel was on fire that year – Jerusalem in particular.

Thursday nights, I would go to the bus station to return home to a place that at the time seemed calmer and safer. The station was hectic and packed with people going home for Shabbat: soldiers, students, and workers, all rushing to end the week. The atmosphere at the station at the time (it was the old open station) was always tense but liberating.

The magic of the Central Bus Station is in its vitality and pace, a fulfillment of the prophecy of Zechariah (8:4–5): "There shall yet old men and old women sit in the broad places of Jerusalem, every man with his staff in his hand for very age. And the broad places of the city shall be full of boys and girls playing in the broad places thereof."

Inbal Arieli

At Home on Metzitzim Beach, Tel Aviv

Inbal Arieli *is a serial entrepreneur and tech influencer, Managing Partner at Big IL, and Board Member at a variety of start-ups and innovation programs. She is the author of* Chutzpah: Why Israel Is a Hub of Innovation and Entrepreneurship.

When I was twenty years old, I moved from my parents' home to Tel Aviv, joining my then boyfriend – who later became my beloved husband – in our first apartment. Having been raised in a family of diverse backgrounds – my father immigrated to Israel from Egypt, my mother from Poland – I immediately felt at home in Tel Aviv with the endless options it offers.

More than anything in this vibrant city, I fell in love with the Mediterranean and its beautiful beaches. They're like sweets in a candy store. Only 550 meters from our apartment, we had a variety of options, representing the diversity of Israeli society: in a short distance, walkable in a few minutes, I could meet people of all kinds. Starting with Metzitzim Beach, my favorite spot in Israel.

An iconic landmark of modern Tel Aviv, this beach is the first along the coastline in the heart of the city, but also one of the first historically. It attracts families due to the playground it offers and the older population because of its easy accessibility. It is filled with people, intensity, and authenticity, which for me is exactly what Tel Aviv is all about. Spring, autumn, summer, or winter, I spend many hours there with my family and friends or by myself. Our soundtrack is the beat of the *matkot* (paddleball racquets), our menu fresh watermelon.

What I like the most about Metzitzim Beach is its coastal neighborhood: right next to Metzitzim, there is a separate beach for ultra-Orthodox bathers with alternate days for men and women; next is the "dog beach," where people bring their dogs to enjoy a sea breeze; then the LGBTQ+ beach, which has become a magnet for the global LGBTQ+ community; the fancier Hilton Beach, with its volleyball and paddleboard clubs; and finally, the wild beach for surfers. All of that diversity in just 500 meters. And so it continues. Just as the Mediterranean itself has no walls, there are no real walls between the personalities of Tel Aviv.

In between investing in tech start-ups, writing *Chutzpah* (my book on the skills of the future), and speaking around the world about Israel's flourishing tech ecosystem, I enjoy my downtime – or should I say balance time – while paddle-boarding or swimming in the sea by Metzitzim Beach. Sometimes I go alone, sometimes with my dogs or with my husband and our three sons. The beautiful view of the water, the evening sunsets, the warmth of the sand, and more than anything, the diversity of people walking by make this the place where I feel at home.

Orit Gadiesh

Lifelong Friendship on the Tel Aviv Beach

The Tel Aviv beach is an integral part of the city and perhaps its most famous "street." It was there before Tel Aviv was born, and it has continued to be central to life in the city through all the ups and downs (British Mandate, the War of Independence, immigration waves). The beach was the site of the first land lottery in what became Tel Aviv, conducted in 1909 with seashells. It was where the first paved street led to. It was where couples went and still go for a walk and young lovers to lose themselves. Where children play and people of all ages swim and socialize. It has been a constant in the village that became a town and grew up to be an amazing city.

Whenever I can, I have a drink or dinner on the beach. Preferably at sunset when the sky becomes a red ball reflected in the blue water, and people become dark silhouettes against that background.

When I was growing up, it was quieter than today. There were only a few coffee shops. Of course, the walks and the playing and swimming and the love affairs were there. On one of those evening walks, a couple with a three-year-old girl stopped to chat with a man walking along with his small daughter. This is one of my earliest memories, most likely because the man only had one arm. The rest of the "memory" was supplied years later by my mother. My father and the other man had fought together in the IDF and before. All three settled down for a long chat. That left the two little girls to show initiative and find common ground to play together. According to my mother, this took the girls two minutes or so, which allowed the grown-ups to talk for almost two hours.

Orit Gadiesh *is Chairman of the global management consulting firm Bain & Company and a renowned expert on management and corporate strategy with over forty years of global experience.*

That beach was where the early foundation of a friendship was laid down. The girls lived in different parts of the city but met in high school again, not remembering the beach encounter. But from then on, a lifetime friendship grew. One that became closer and more profound as years passed – even though we have lived most of our adult years geographically apart.

My very good friend Smadar and I never lost our love of beaches. Or of each other.

Photos: Gil Shwed

Photo: Ron Kedmi

Aki Avni is one of the most respected artists of cinema, television, and theater for the last three decades in Israel. Aki has been acting, directing, and producing films and television series for many years and has won many Academy Awards for his work. He lives with his wife Nicole and his children in Israel.

Aki Avni

Coming Alive at Habima National Theater

My grandfather Ya'akov was the spark and the inspiration that got me into the spirit of performing arts. He would take me on three buses from Rehovot to Tel Aviv for the biweekly rehearsals for the Young Talents Festival in which I was taking part. Every time we passed by the Habima National Theater in the heart of Tel Aviv, my breath would catch. Through the eyes of a twelve-year-old boy, this looked like Mount Sinai, with me as Moses looking toward the Chosen Land yet never able to enter it.

My eleventh-grade class went to see the play *Accidental Death of an Anarchist* at Habima. The big city and the huge theater building, a monument to the glory of theatrical arts and drama standing in a place of honor right in the middle of the city, filled my heart with endless excitement.

The curtain lifted. I had never been so transfixed as in those crucial two hours of my life, and the decision was immediate: this is where I belong, this is the home of my heart, here I want to live, and for this my soul longs.

After the play, I decided to have a look around the impressive, vast building. I slipped away behind the stairs leading to the foyer, and from there to the rehearsal studio. The costumes, the props, the model stage, and the actors reading their lines in the rehearsal next door fascinated me.

I continued my walk through the building. On the walls hung pictures of the founders, a group of actors who had founded the Habima Theater in Moscow under the guidance of Stanislavsky, the great creator of the modern acting method. In 1918, they arrived in Israel as a group to reestablish the theater in Tel Aviv. At the end of the corridor, I reached a large door and opened it to discover the theater's small auditorium. One ray of light fell on the stage. I could hear the actors' voices and watch them performing, and the feeling that I had arrived home deepened.

Returning to the hallway, I saw another door with the little sign "Habima Archive." I entered a time tunnel of Israeli

Photo: Natalie Arviv

Photos: Elitzur

culture: hundreds of documents, thousands of photographs from hundreds of plays with thousands of actors in an imaginary world that overwhelmed me.

I realized it was really late. Oh, no, had I forgotten myself? I ran out of the theater to find my schoolmates assembled by the bands playing in the square outside. There was so much talent, and the inspiration the building gave them was palpable, as though it encouraged them to sharpen their gifts.

When I graduated from the Yoram Loewenstein Performing Arts Studio after three inspiring yet grueling years of theater studies, I received a phone call. On the line was Haim Sela, the lead producer of the Habima National Theater. "Come to the theater tomorrow morning; we want to offer you something," he said. I did not sleep a wink all night.

In the morning I walked into the vast building. Behind a small desk in a small office sat Haim Sela.

"When did you finish your studies?"

"This very week."

"Then you haven't worked in a theater yet?"

"Not yet."

"We wanted to offer you Tony, the lead in West Side Story."

Flash forward. As I rode my bike through this beautiful and lively city to the dress rehearsal at the theater, I could feel the amazing spirit of art permeating every corner of this city that lives and breathes culture: from the Charles Bronfman Auditorium to the Habima National Theater.

I had to hurry to rehearsal, as that night the play premiered. Before the first performance of my career in theater, I climbed the ladder in the wings of the central auditorium the Rubina Hall. I got onto the lighting bridge above the stage, feeling like the Phantom of the Opera. Standing there, looking at the thousand-person-strong audience, I was filled with gratitude to and appreciation of Grandpa Ya'akov, who had given me the love for acting and the desire to be in the actors' world.

My grandpa himself was an actor but was not accepted to Habima. I am continuing his path in this city and in Israel's center for theater – the Habima National Theater.

Julia Zaher is the CEO of Al Arz Tahini, an internationally successful family business in Nazareth that proudly withstood backlash after donating to help fund a hotline for Arabic-speaking LGBTQ Israelis.

Julia Zaher

Nazareth Market: The Pearl of Nazareth

As a child, my favorite thing to do was accompanying my mother to the *shuk* (market) to shop. In the Nazareth of old, there were no shops on the main street – all the stores were inside the market. It was the bustling center of the city, all day and all week long.

I remember that there was a pharmacy there, the only one in the region. The owner was a pharmacist who used to prepare his own creams, and all the women in the city would buy his face cream.

The Nazareth market was special, as it had shops for many occupations that unfortunately, we no longer find today. One man polished copper pots, for example. Another sharpened knives, up until just recently. Another made handmade kitchen implements from aluminum.

The market was constructed of beautiful homes, most made of stone, with stunning paintings on the ceilings. Today one can take a tour of the ceilings in the Old City of Nazareth. The homes were built on two floors – the ground floor was for commerce, while the top floor was the living space. The business owners lived above their stores.

These old homes had a living room with a large divan in the middle, with the other rooms surrounding it. The divan was where the family sat together, and it was also used for entertaining. Of course, there was no television, and customarily, in the evenings, the father of the family would sit on the divan with his family and tell stories. Most of the wealthy families lived there in the Old City. Muslims and Christians lived together in harmony, as good neighbors.

In the past, the families were large and friendly. The women would boast about their cooking. They would take platters of their special dishes around to the neighbors. The traditional dish in Nazareth was *kibbeh nayyeh* – raw meat with a special spice mixture. The recipe is still preserved, and everyone gives it a personal twist.

The entrances to the homes were decorated with greenery, mainly basil and lily fruit that the residents planted in tin cans.

Every day of the week, but especially on Fridays, people would travel to Nazareth from the surrounding villages, sometimes on organized buses, to go shopping. You could even buy camels, donkeys, and goats.

In time, many stores opened on the main road. People bought cars, and it became easier to go shopping outside the market. This led to a decline in the number of visitors, and businesses closed. Eventually, the entire market closed and became a ghost town...but its beauty remains. The families who lived there sold their homes and moved to neighborhoods outside the Old City.

For years, this pearl, the former market, was neglected. But a few years ago, some women from Nazareth decided to revive it by opening stores, each in their own particular field. Today we are witnessing a renewal of small businesses, mainly women artists who have opened galleries to present their works.

They are engravers, embroiderers, and painters. Mainly, they are attempting to reconstruct and preserve the old Nazareth style of art. Visitors can enjoy lovely cafes with traditional snacks as well as shops selling vegetables and meat.

The Church of the Annunciation is located inside the market, with the Synagogue Church adjacent to it, attracting visitors from Israel and around the world. In addition, many authentic-style guest houses and hostels have been opened, where tourists can discover the special atmosphere. I invite you to come take a specialty tour focusing on topics such as food, culture, and art, or meet with residents to hear their stories and experience Nazareth like a local.

Chemi Peres

Kinneret Cemetery: In Loving Memory of Guy Peres

Chemi Peres *is a venture capital and innovation pioneer and serves as the Chairman of the Board of Directors of the Peres Center for Peace and Innovation, Israel's leading nonprofit organization, established in 1996 by his late father, Israel's ninth President and former Prime Minister Shimon Peres.*

The symbolic meanings of landscapes are often hidden to us, and more so their personal meanings. Such is the case of the Kinneret cemetery, an enchanting burial ground at the foot of the Sea of Galilee.

This beautiful and serene cemetery, sometimes referred to as the Pantheon of the Labor Party, is the eternal home of some of Israel's most iconic Zionist pioneers. Officially, it serves as a burial site for the inhabitants of the region's first two communities, Kibbutz Kvutzat Kinneret, founded in 1914, and Moshava Kinneret, founded in 1908, both located just across the road. But many Jewish pioneers and non-pioneers are buried here as well, making it an attractive site for visitors seeking to explore their collective ideological identity, as well as those seeking personal refuge.

Those who are familiar with traditional Jewish cemeteries will appreciate the uniqueness of this cemetery. From the surrounding mountains to the beautiful Kinneret lake, the prolific and exotic vegetation, and the relative location and appearance of the tombstones, everything here expresses a depth of meaning and a liberty of the spirit.

In a traditional Jewish cemetery, for example, graves are arranged according to the chronological order of the burial, but not so with the Kinneret cemetery, where adjacent graves might indicate a time difference of several decades. A touching example is the grave of the political leader and pioneer Berl Katznelson (1887–1944), who was at the center of a celebrated love triangle with his first love, Sarah Shmukler (1889–1919), who is buried to his right, and his wife, Leah Miron (1888–1967), buried to his left.

Customary Hebrew inscriptions for Jewish headstones are rarely found here. Some inscriptions are engraved in the handwriting of the deceased, an informal quality that creates an immediate sense of intimacy. In others, we find an unorthodox deviation from traditional Jewish epitaphs. One example of both the former and the latter is the grave

The late Guy Peres at the Academy of Arts in San Francisco

Kinneret Cemetery - Chemi Peres

of author and playwright Aharon Megged. Here the customary lettering ".ת.נ.צ.ב.ה," which forms the acronym for "May his soul be bound up in the bond of life," has been paraphrased to say "His soul is bound up in his books" – a clever wordplay that beautifully captures the author's personality and life's work.

Kinneret cemetery thus holds a certain tolerance toward death and mourning rituals. It is a place where restrictive traditions are not necessarily observed, which offers visitors the opportunity to look at the lives – rather than the deaths – of the people buried here.

Indeed, Kinneret cemetery is brimming with stories. Among those buried here are legendary Zionist leaders such as Nachman Syrkin, Ber Borochov, Moses Hess, Avraham Herzfeld, and Shmuel Stoller, as well as some of our nation's most beloved poets, authors, and thinkers, such as Naomi Shemer, who gave us the eternal gift of song, imbued with her love for the land.

Kinneret Cemetery
(all photos: Chemi Peres)

A few steps away, we find the grave of Rachel, another venerated Hebrew poetess. Hers tells the painfully romantic story of a young pioneer and of her tragic death from tuberculosis at the age of forty. In her short life, Rachel became known for her simple yet exceedingly lyrical style. In many of her poems, she mourns the life she never had, expressing intense feelings of longing and loss. A book of her hugely popular poems can be found in a stainless steel container attached to her grave. Echoing through the cemetery, her poems simultaneously lament the dead and celebrate their lives.

Perhaps *by Rachel*
(translated from Hebrew by A.C. Jacobs)[1]

Perhaps it was never so.

Perhaps

I never woke early and went to the fields

To labor in the sweat of my brow

Nor in the long blazing days

Of harvest

On top of the wagon laden with sheaves,

Made my voice ring with song

Nor bathed myself clean in the calm

Blue water

Of my Kinneret. O, my Kinneret,

Were you there or did I only dream?

On March 20, 2022, the Kinneret cemetery embraced another tragic member into its bosom. Guy Peres, beloved son of Gila and Chemi and brother of Nadav and Yael, passed away at the age of thirty-three. His headstone, like his art, tells a story of a life rich in color, imagination, passion, and meaning. No other burial ground but the Kinneret cemetery could ever contain a personality so liberated, so devoted to self-expression, and so creative. Here, his soul is bound up in the memory of his loved ones and of all those who would have loved him. His works and dreams light our lives; he is forever in our hearts.

---

1 Shemuel Yeshayahu Penueli and Azriel Ukhmani, *Anthology of Modern Hebrew Poetry* (Jerusalem: Institute for the Translation of Hebrew Literature and Israel Universities Press, 1966).

PART VI

EDUCATION AND SPORTS
Excellence of the Mind and Body

Photo: Amit Gabay-Murvitz

Avichai (Avi) Kremer

Vitality at the Technion

Avichai (Avi) Kremer is a graduate of the Technion and of Harvard Business School. He is a cofounder of the nonprofit organization Prize4Life, which is dedicated to the discovery of treatments and a cure for amyotrophic lateral sclerosis (ALS). He has been living with ALS for close to two decades.

The Technion – Israel Institute of Technology is located in Haifa, my hometown, on Mount Carmel. The Technion is the equivalent of MIT for Israel, the "start-up nation." It's a place where cutting-edge research is developed, and the technology of the future is tested in the labs.

The Technion is also the first university in Israel, established in 1912, over a hundred years ago and thirty-six years before Israel itself existed. At the time, the modern Hebrew language wasn't spoken, and the decision of the Technion to teach engineering in Hebrew (instead of German, which was then considered the standard scientific language) was a turning point in the revival of a dead language.

Indeed, the Technion's 100,000-plus alumni are the backbone of Israel's highly successful high tech and life science industries. I am one of those alumni, as are my father and siblings. Academically, those were the most demanding years of my life. Nevertheless, the Technion doesn't only set high standards for its students. The exceptional thing I was taught there was *how to learn.*

Another thing that is unique about the Technion is its great atmosphere of coexistence. The city of Haifa itself is considered an inspiring model of coexistence between Arabs and Jews. In every department of the Technion, one can hear Arabic alongside Hebrew in the classes and laboratories, food courts and dorms. Because at the Technion, everyone is Israeli and enters by merit.

As mentioned earlier, the Technion is located on Mount Carmel, in the north of Israel. Mount Carmel is known as the "evergreen mountain," and the Technion campus is immersed in nature, full of green areas, trees, grass, and flowers. The beautiful view of Haifa Bay and the Mediterranean Sea is visible from almost every point of the campus.

Like the country of Israel itself, the Technion campus is a mix between old and new; some of the campus buildings predate the country, but most are modern. Sculptures and man-made waterfalls are scattered throughout the campus. There is always something special going on.

What I remember most from my years at the Technion is the tremendous rapport among the students. Many academic assignments are done in groups, and even those that are individual are so difficult that one could use a friendly pointer on a regular basis. Before final exams, we used to hold mini-marathon group studies. The reasoning behind this group process is that it resembles the process at workplaces, especially start-ups. Indeed, numerous start-ups originated with these friendships forged at the Technion among classmates. My greatest asset from the Technion is the friends I have made there. Frankly, I doubt if I would have graduated without them.

Walking through the campus, one can simply feel the energy. Young people are all around, in their prime, seeking education and dreaming of making a difference in the world. With 70 percent of Israeli high tech founders and managers being Technion alumni, innovation and entrepreneurship are in the air! The finest future innovators of Israel – maybe the world – are walking in the corridors on the way to yet another cutting-edge technology class, grabbing something to eat in the cafeteria, or relaxing on the grass. This vibrant atmosphere is one of two main reasons I love coming back to visit my alma mater (the other is my fond memories, of course).

For me, the Technion represents the best of Israel. A mix between old and new, coexistence of Arabs and Jews, beautiful nature, interesting architecture, an ancient language revived, superb education, cutting-edge research, youthful potential, vibrant energy, friendliness and rapport, creativity and innovation, global impact, and most of all – the spirit of entrepreneurship. The Technion is Israel's past, present and future. Its alumni are the core of Israel's engineering and science fields, as well as management and entrepreneurship. If Israel is the "start-up nation," the Technion is its beating heart. My years there were defining, and the place is special and dear to me.

I invite you to visit the Technion's campus and the beautiful city of Haifa where it resides. Organized tours can be scheduled online at the website of the David and Janet Polak Visitors Center, https://www.technion.ac.il/en/david-and-janet-polak-visitors-center/.

Professor Shulamit Levenberg is the director of both the Technion Center for 3D Bioprinting and the Rina and Avner Schneur Center for Diabetes Research, and holds the Stanley and Sylvia Shirvan Chair in Cancer and Life Sciences in the Faculty of Biomedical Engineering.

Shulamit Levenberg

The Pioneering Spirit at the Faculty of Biomedical Engineering, the Technion

For the past eighteen years, I have had the privilege of calling the Technion's Faculty of Biomedical Engineering my second home. As a professor in the faculty and head of its Stem Cell and Tissue Engineering Laboratory, I love my work and truly enjoy coming to our beautiful campus every day. Perched on Mount Carmel in the scenic port city of Haifa in northern Israel, the Technion – Israel Institute of Technology is home to a large community of outstanding students and researchers from diverse backgrounds who all share a thirst for knowledge and a passion for innovative research.

The cutting-edge science taking place at the Technion in general, and within my faculty in particular, epitomizes what I love most about Israel: its pioneering spirit and determination to reshape and improve our world. It is exciting to be part of this community and to be able to apply my expertise in tissue engineering to help heal damaged organs and tissues by developing techniques to implant engineered grafts.

Biomedical engineering offers endless developmental directions, from diagnosis to treatment to the enhancement of medicine and healthcare. The Technion's Faculty of Biomedical Engineering aims to maximize the integration of science and engineering to improve quality of life for people around the world. In recent years, the field has generated a wealth of research-related start-ups and opportunities; consequently, there has been a significant surge in the number of students pursuing this field of study.

As Israel's largest biomedical engineering faculty, our department is the driving force for building both a national and an international community of scientists and engineers equipped with practical knowledge and capabilities to better understand medical problems and develop strategies and technologies to solve them.

One of the priorities of the Faculty of Biomedical Engineering is to meet the growing need to streamline and provide solutions to the medical industry in the research and development of new medical technologies. To this end, it brings together diverse theoretical and experimental research areas such as medical imaging, nano-mechanics, molecular medicine, tissue engineering, neuroengineering, and more.

The research conducted in my lab strives to find advanced solutions for a variety of medical conditions. For example, we research stem cell–based therapies for treating spinal cord injuries as well as the effect of vascularization on spinal cord regeneration. We have also achieved breakthroughs in bone tissue repair: we engineer defect-specific grafts made of biocompatible biomaterials and implant them in order to regenerate complex bone tissue. In another project, we take an innovative approach to helping patients with type 2 diabetes. Skeletal muscle cells are genetically modified to construct engineered muscle tissue, which, when implanted, decreases the glucose levels in diabetics.

Recently, my lab has succeeded in printing the world's first slaughter-free ribeye steak, together with our start-up Aleph Farms. This was accomplished using three-dimensional bioprinting technology and the natural building blocks of meat – real cow cells. In 2018, we unveiled the world's first cultivated thin-cut steak, and we now have the ability to print any structure of slaughter-free steak. This development has great potential, and my lab plans to continue exploring useful applications for advanced tissue engineering.

The faculty maintains a close relationship with industry and the healthcare system in order to better understand the needs in the field and to create an implementable interface for the technological transfer of ideas stemming from the faculty's labs. In addition to Aleph Farms, research from my lab has generated two other promising start-ups: NurExone, which offers a new approach for treating spinal cord injuries; and Nanosynex, which provides new solutions to improve and speed up diagnostic processes.

The Faculty of Biomedical Engineering is just one of seventeen academic faculties offering undergraduate and graduate degrees at Israel's premier research university. The university houses over sixty research centers, many of them multidisciplinary, including the Russell Berrie Nanotechnology Institute, the Nancy and Stephen Grand Technion Energy Program, and the Helen Diller Quantum Center. It is an honor to be a member of the Technion's faculty, which includes numerous winners of prestigious prizes and three Nobel Prize laureates.

In this age of globalization, the Technion is becoming an increasingly international institution. Every year, Technion International welcomes a large community of international students from all over the world for short-term programs or for entire degree studies, including many post-doc fellows.

I am always proud to share my "second home" with visitors and to show guests the Technion's state-of-the-art facilities and cutting-edge research projects. Visitors can also learn more about the university's history and current activities at the newly renovated David and Janet Polak Visitors Center. I hope to see you on campus!

Arik Ze'evi

The Best of Israel at the Wingate Institute

Arik Ze'evi *is an Olympic medal–winning dan 6 black belt in Judo. Today he is retired from competition and is a lecturer and consultant.*

The Wingate Institute is Israel's National Institute for Sport Excellence. It is situated in one of the most beautiful areas in Israel, atop a ridge on the Poleg seafront, on the southern border of Netanya.

I chose Wingate Institute primarily because I spent most of my athletic career there. My first visit was at the age of twelve to train with Israel's national youth Judo team. The training took place once a week, on Tuesday afternoons, and I remember how I used to rush home from school, eat in haste, pack my bag, and set out for the institute.

The trip from my home in Bnei Brak to the door of the institute involved two buses along the Coastal Highway, after which I had to walk another fifteen to twenty minutes before finding myself in the Judo training facility on the western edge of campus.

Later in my career I trained there twice or even three times a week, and eventually after graduating high school at the age of eighteen and a half, I moved into the student dorms there. From then on, all of my training took place on campus.

The time I spent living there was undoubtedly the best period of my life. Not only was I beginning an independent life, but it was centered on the sport I love. I felt like a true professional, and I also got to enjoy the excellent facilities at Wingate: a physiotherapy center, a cafeteria, a sauna and jacuzzi to restore energy, and the country's largest training hall, as well as proximity to the sea, a beautiful view, an excellent location between Herzliya and Netanya, and most importantly, living next to my teammates and athletes in other fields.

170 My Israel

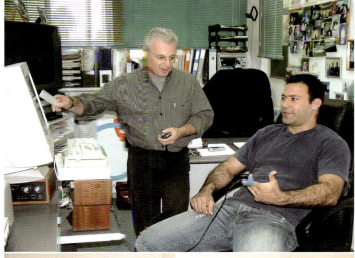

I lived at Wingate for four years, but even having left the dorms and moved elsewhere in Israel, I continued returning there daily. Every time I set foot on campus, I felt suffused with an impossible combination of serenity and tension. This sensation never left me, even up to the very last time I entered the institute as an Olympic athlete.

Yet the essential reason I chose the Wingate Institute to symbolize my Israel is that it represents what I would call Israel's most beautiful face. It is a place of excellence that allows in a very real way for the truest possible integration. In sports, your race, gender, or origin plays no part, as you are only measured by your athletic ability. Wingate Institute is home to athletes of every description.

I came to the national team from the Pardes Katz neighborhood, a very bad area, then even considered criminal. With me on the team were boys from Tel Aviv, Ra'anana, Petach Tikva, and Haifa, children from moshavim and kibbutzim, and even two boys who came all the way from Eilat. But nobody cared, because our only measure was our success in the sport.

This integration took place not only in my field – it was felt everywhere.

In the dorm next to mine lived an Ethiopian athlete, a marathon runner who represented us in Athens in 2004. On the other side lived an Arab wrestler from Be'er Sheva; in the room across from me was Eitan Orbach, the Olympic swimmer from Haifa, and next to him was a female athlete who had recently immigrated from the USSR. At Wingate, you could meet people from every sector of society.

To some extent, Wingate represents Israel at its best. It promotes health, sportsmanship, and excellence. It welcomes people from all over Israel, giving them the opportunity to try to be the absolute best in their fields. And it does all this with the best view in the world – the Mediterranean seaside.

This is why, to me, Wingate Institute is the most beautiful representation of Israel. Or perhaps it is better to say that Wingate represents Israel the way I would like to see it.

Photo: Eric Sultan

Professor Ronit Satchi-Fainaro is Director of TAU's Cancer Research and Nanomedicine Laboratory, Head of TAU's Cancer Biology Research Center, Head of the TAU Kahn 3D BioPrinting Initiative, and Chair of the Department of Physiology and Pharmacology at the Sackler Faculty of Medicine.

Ronit Satchi-Fainaro

Multidisciplinary Diversity at Tel Aviv University

Tel Aviv University (TAU) is a microcosm of all that I love about Israel – socially, academically, technologically, and culturally.

Located at the heart of Israel's high-tech and business center, within the "city that never sleeps," TAU represents Israel at its best. It is dynamic, innovative, cosmopolitan, and forward-looking. From its humble beginnings in 1956, TAU has evolved into Israel's largest and most diversified university, with 130 schools and departments that span the spectrum of sciences, humanities, and arts. Its beautiful and verdant campus is home to 1,000 research groups spread through nine faculties; 18 performing arts centers; 27 schools; 340 research centers; 400 labs; a botanic garden with 4,000 plant species; a research zoo with 220 species of mammals, birds, and reptiles; and so much more. With over 30,000 students, it is the largest university in the country.

According to the 2019 Global Innovation Index, Israel ranks first in the world for research talent in business enterprise and second for university-industry research collaboration. TAU – a Reuters Top 100 Innovation University rated first in Israel for US patents (NAI and IPO) – is the main force behind these national rankings. TAU researchers and alumni were responsible for no fewer than seven of the twelve Israeli inventions and companies cited by the *Times of Israel* as having changed the world in the last decade. These include Waze, the Iron Dome missile defense system, the SpaceIL moonshot (Beresheet), Mobileye, and the first-ever 3D-printed live heart and 3D-bioprinted human cancer models for personalized medicine. Truly something to be proud of.

For me, one of TAU's most special features is its inherently multidisciplinary and collaborative research culture. With no barriers between the disciplines, the possibilities for academic creativity are infinite –

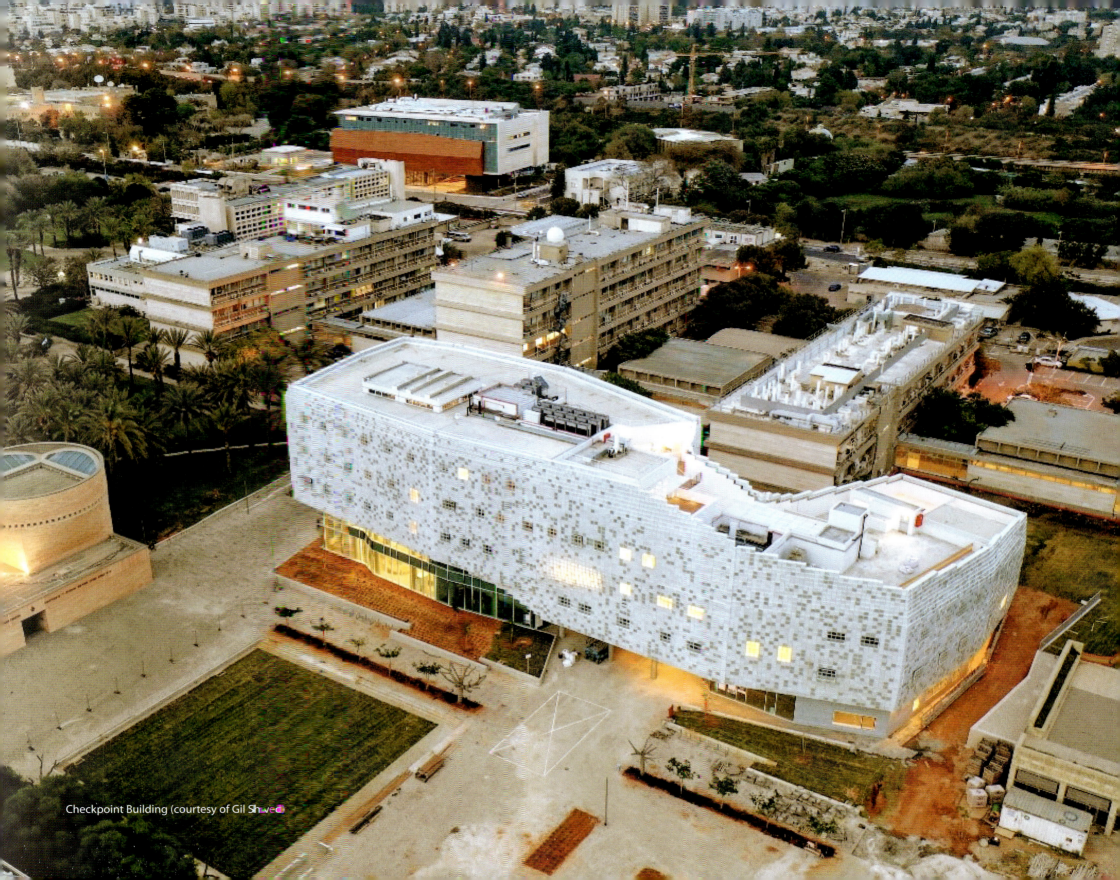

Checkpoint Building (courtesy of Gil Shwed)

enabling, for example, biblical archaeologists to work with physicists, neurologists to work with management scholars, physicians to work with architects, engineers to work with occupational therapists. Indeed, at my lab, which is based in the medical faculty, the team comprises biologists, chemists, clinicians, engineers, nano-scientists and computer scientists – bio-convergence at its best.

When wandering around the TAU campus, one will also notice its truly international nature. The university has cooperative agreements with over 280 institutions in forty-six countries, and its labs regularly host overseas researchers. It frequently receives delegations of statesmen, intellectuals, academics, businesspeople, and cultural personalities from across the globe. In addition, over twenty-two hundred students from a hundred countries enroll in diverse study programs at TAU's international school every year.

I'm proud to say that the university's diverse and multihued student body represents the entire spectrum of Israeli society: Jews study alongside Muslim and Christian Arabs, Orthodox alongside secular, native Israelis alongside overseas students, and the disabled alongside their able-bodied peers. This cosmopolitan and pluralistic campus culture ensures an intellectually, culturally, and socially enriching experience for residents and visitors alike.

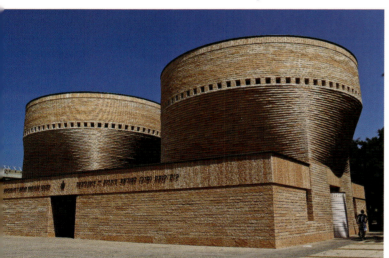

TAU Cymbalista Jewish Heritage Center (courtesy of TAU)

Among the iconic facilities well worth the visit are those dedicated to the study of medicine and biology. One such place is the Sackler Faculty of Medicine. Home to more than four thousand alumni – Israel's largest concentration of scientists and clinicians – investigating all aspects of human health and disease, the Sackler Faculty of Medicine and its seventeen affiliated medical centers form the backbone of Israel's medical establishment.

Another impressive building is the Blavatnik Center for Drug Discovery. I serve on the advisory board of this state-of-the-art facility – a unique place where biology, chemistry, and computer science combine to deepen knowledge and advance lab breakthroughs toward the stage where they are ripe for commercial development.

For animal lovers, the Steinhardt Museum of Natural History – part of the National Center for Biodiversity Studies – is a priceless national treasure with over 5.5 million specimens of animals and plants that tell the story of the Middle East over the past centuries.

Tech enthusiasts will appreciate the Abramovich Building for Nanoscience and Nanotechnology. Currently under construction, this building will be the permanent home of TAU's nano center. The building will form a spectacular new entrance to the university, right next to ANU – Museum of the Jewish People.

The Check Point Building is another impressive site. This five-thousand-square-meter building is home to two TAU units: the Blavatnik School of Computer Science (ranked in the world's top twenty) and the Youth University, a framework that brings schoolchildren from across Israel to the campus to garner scientific knowledge and develop intellectual skills.

There are countless more places to explore, but I leave you with the architectural gem that is the Cymbalista Synagogue and Jewish Heritage Center. The synagogue was created with a dual purpose: to house a synagogue and to bridge the gap between religious and secular segments of Israeli society in an academic environment. A masterpiece designed by world-renowned Swiss architect Mario Botta, it is undoubtedly one of the most striking edifices in Israel.

Yael Arad

The Fight for Excellence at Maccabi Tel Aviv

Yael Arad *is a celebrated judoka and the first Israeli to bring home an Olympic medal, taking silver in Barcelona in 1992 and gold in the 1993 European championships, as well as multiple other medals throughout her career. She is a business consultant and motivational speaker, as well as President of the Olympic Committee of Israel.*

My club, Maccabi Tel Aviv, stood at 4 Maccabi Street, right on top of the old Orly Cinema. The building backed onto the colorful Bezalel Market, with its felafel stands and hawkers. From our window, we had a view of the special atmosphere of King George Street – noisy buses exhaling black fumes, busy kiosks, simple food joints, and bakeries with hot rugelach and the best poppy seed pastries around.

My club was an island of competitive sports at a time when Olympic sports hadn't yet become a point of national pride for Israel. In the late 1970s, there were only two sports in Israel: soccer and basketball – Tal Brody, Miki Berkovich, and Motti Aroesti; Jim Boatwright, Lou Silver, and Aulcie Perry; plus Mordechai Spiegler and Giora Spiegel. Other sports hadn't reached the Israeli consciousness – they were only recognized by those in the know.

Our club did have tennis courts, plus a basketball court where legendary players and coaches held their practice sessions – Tanchum Cohen-Mintz, Ralph Klein, Yehoshua Rozin, and many more. Our building was named after David Berger, the champion weightlifter who was one of the Israeli athletes massacred in the 1972 terror attack at the Munich Olympics. There was a weight room downstairs on the ground floor, and the judo hall was on the top floor.

For me and a group of kids from the Tel Aviv area, the club became our second home. Every day, we'd meet there for practice, and we became close friends.

After school, I would rush home to eat lunch and get my bag ready for practice. Then I'd walk

Photo: Ilan Bsor

176 My Israel

to the bus stop for the 24 and 42 lines that took me to the club. I remember racing to the bus stop so I wouldn't miss my bus.

The minute I arrived at our club, I entered another world. I crossed the crooked tiles of the outdoor basketball court and said hi to Amnon, the maintenance man. After waving to the tennis instructors, I'd enter the weight room, where I watched Shoni, Barak, and Oren lifting weights many times their own body weight. They'd invite me, a little girl of twelve, to try my hand at the weights. They taught me techniques and slapped my shoulder to wish me success at practice.

Up on the second floor, I'd meet up with Moni Aizik, my trainer since childhood, charismatic but strict, and the rest of my group – mostly boys and a few girls. We got dressed in the rear courtyard, and then we'd tie on our belts – first yellow, then orange, green, and blue, our expressions serious and self-important. Then we'd joke around a bit before settling down to an intense, two-hour workout.

Moni treated us like professional athletes, a special forces unit – and we repaid him with total dedication.

After I joined the Israeli national team and my daily workouts moved to the Wingate Institute, I still practiced at the Tel Aviv club twice a week until I retired. Maccabi Tel Aviv was my professional home – it was there that I felt unconditional acceptance.

Over time, real estate prices in Tel Aviv skyrocketed, and the Bezalel Market area was placed under private development. It took years, but eventually the Orly Cinema was torn down. The tennis courts were next to go, and the area became a busy parking lot. Our building was the last holdout – but finally its turn came as well, and our old judo group held a farewell party in its honor.

Today the site holds luxury apartments, cafes, and an underground parking garage. Of course, it's normal and even understandable that this valuable piece of real estate in the heart of Tel Aviv would be renovated. But every time I pass by, I go back to being little Yael from Tel Aviv with the yellow or blue belt. I smell the familiar tang of sweat from the judo hall. I hear the basketball coach downstairs shouting at the kids and the booms of hundreds of pounds of weights crashing to the floor – and I dream of becoming a true champion. The simple restaurants may have been replaced by student pubs, but my beloved Weiss Bakery is still there, with the aroma of rugelach in the air and the best poppy seed pastries in town.

But all this pales alongside the values of excellence, determination, and mutual respect that I learned, and the lifetime friendships that I made with the other kids from 4 Maccabi Street – my club, Maccabi Tel Aviv.

Shirin Natour-Hafi

The Vision at ORT School for Science and Engineering, Lod

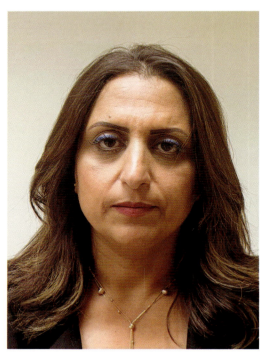

Shirin Natour-Hafi is the Principal of the first state Arab ORT School, located in the Rakevet neighborhood of Lod. In 2013, she was chosen as a member of the World Economic Forum (WEF)'s Young Global Leaders, a selective cohort of young professionals from all over the world.

At the heart of the city of Lod lies the Rakevet neighborhood, a half-forgotten place complicated by its socioeconomic status. It is one of Israel's most divided neighborhoods, and as such it is prone to riots. For the youth living here, hardship, discrimination, and disorder are a fact of life. It was this reality that I stepped into thirteen years ago to be principal of the first state Arab high school, the ORT School for Science and Engineering.

I was born just two blocks away from where ORT is today and left the neighborhood at an early age to join a Jewish high school, where I was the only Arab. After graduating from Bar-Ilan University, I spent the next fourteen years as a teacher of Hebrew literature at a Jewish high school. By the time I got back to Rakevet, I had become an outsider in my own town.

In 2009, when I agreed to take on the challenge of establishing the school, I was a thirty-four-year-old Muslim woman with a pristine Hebrew accent and no hijab, about to take on a traditional male role in a place where religion and conservatism still rule. Despite the many objections and concerns, I was determined to return home to fight for the important vision of giving the Rakevet youth a chance at a better future.

Today, where once was an olive grove stands one of the finest structures in the city. The ORT campus features spacious classes, a library, an auditorium, and multiple laboratories filled with state-of-the-art equipment. In all its beauty, the school sometimes seems to me like a healthy lung amidst a black forest of neglected traffic arteries. The building itself is a symbol of the value we place on education, designed to send a message to our students that we love them and are willing to invest every resource available to us in their future.

Our fifteen hundred students have access to the most advanced study programs and initiatives, some of which are the first of their kind in Israel. One example is a special program we offer in cooperation with the Schwartz/

Reisman Institute for Theoretical Physics at the Weizmann Institute of Science, where students learn alongside some of Israel's top scientists and researchers. There are also dozens of enhanced classes in finance and banking, citizenship, Israel's legal system, architecture, English, biology, chemistry, early childhood education, engineering, electrical engineering, communications, agriculture and environmental science, computer science, business management, and many more.

We have been blessed with a fleet of devoted volunteers who support our vision and are committed to it. These include dozens of university students as well as some of Israel's top industry leaders, who have been contributing their time and knowledge to the school on a regular basis for years. Even through the hardest of riots, these volunteers continue to show up, proving to the Rakevet youth that they are a valuable part of society and that there are people who truly care about them.

This might sound banal to anyone who has not known a lifetime of discrimination, but not so for the Rakevet youth, who, as a minority, often feel inferior. Coming from the same background, I can relate. But my experience outside the neighborhood has taught me otherwise. It has shown me that the Arab-Jewish story is only one of many stories. Although it may seem at times like the epicenter of all that is wrong in Israeli society, it is not. There are other divides that need mending, other wrongs to correct.

As principal, I believe it is my duty to show the Rakevet youth that they are not alone in their struggle and that the power to change things for the better is in their hands. I realize that many will not live to see this change. But their children – and their children's children – will enjoy the fruits of their labor.

By now, ORT Lod has become much more than a school; it has become a place where the face of society is shaped. Education will determine the future of our country, which is why I see the educator's role as a calling, one that requires us to see decades into the future. In 2009, establishing ORT Lod was a wild vision. Today, it is one of the sanest, safest, and most welcoming places in Lod. That is a true testament to the great role that education plays in our lives..

Photo: Hadar Dolan

Ruth Polachek is a serial entrepreneur in the tech arena and former Director of Citibank's FinTech Accelerator. The goal of her community of Israeli female software developers, she codes, is to have 50 percent female software developers in the tech industry.

Ruth Polachek

Boosting High Tech at the Hebrew University of Jerusalem

Visiting Hebrew University's campuses is like taking a tour of Israel. There are six different locations, ranging from the Robert H. Smith Faculty of Agriculture and the Koret School of Veterinary Medicine in Rehovot in central Israel to the Interuniversity Institute for Marine Sciences in the resort town of Eilat, and in between, the three main campuses in Jerusalem, our eternal capital, the beating heart of Israel. These include Mount Scopus, Givat Ram/Safra Campus, and the renowned Hebrew University Hadassah Medical School in Ein Kerem.

The Hebrew University of Jerusalem (HUJI) was Israel's first university and part of the Zionist vision laid out at the Katowice Convention in 1884. In 1918, the cornerstones were placed, and soon after, luminaries such as Albert Einstein, Sigmund Freud, and Martin Buber helped promote the establishment of an academic institution in the nascent Jewish settlement. HUJI consistently stars in international rankings of universities among the top one hundred academic institutions in the world, and a great majority of Israel Prize winners and Israeli Nobel laureates are HUJI alumni and faculty members.

While math and science students at Givat Ram/Safra Campus often mock their humanities-minded classmates at Mount Scopus ("the Grass Sciences"), for me and many of my friends, it's where my dreams and hopes for my future started running wild. I remember walking through the Social Sciences Faculty corridor, aware of the fact that I still didn't know anyone and hadn't yet launched my career, but I knew that the field of possibility was open to me if I only reached out to grasp it. Hebrew U allowed me to widen my horizons and expand my opportunities, even though I knew nothing yet about what was to come. I was, however, confident that I was gaining the knowledge and training to take on whatever would come next.

182 My Israel

In 2008, as part of the Asper Center for Entrepreneurship, I founded a club for HU alumni called eClub HUJI. We invited leading Israeli start-up founders to talk with alumni about their career paths. Today, this club and others like it are housed within Asper-HUJI Innovate, HUJI's vibrant center for innovation and entrepreneurship.

In 2013, I founded she codes to help women integrate into and advance in the high-tech world. The first branch was at Google Campus in Tel Aviv. Later, when I decided I wanted to bring she codes to university campuses, there was no question in my mind as to which university would be my first academic branch. Now, we have over fifty branches across the country – and at all the universities – that train and place women in software engineering positions and help them advance to senior positions in the tech field.

Why did I choose to go to Hebrew U? Well, I never really had much say in the matter. My grandfather retired as Chief of Medicine at a VA hospital to make aliyah and work as a physician in the Pulmonary Department of Hebrew University Hadassah Medical School. My father spent his junior year abroad at the Hebrew U's International School when the Mount Scopus Campus was inaccessible following Israel's War of Independence in 1948 (it didn't reopen until 1968, after the Six-Day War). My older brother and sister also went to Hebrew U – he to the Law School and she to Givat Ram/Safra Campus. Therefore, deciding where to go for college was a no-brainer; the only question was which campus.

Places to check out:

- **Givat Ram/Safra Campus**. This is definitely the most beautiful of Hebrew U's campuses. "The Aquarium" is the infamous computer science students' computer and hangout room, where students remain day and night to complete their gory tasks. Asper HUJI Innovate features *she codes*. Come for one of our hackathons or coding-skills lectures. The National Library is home to every manuscript and book published in Israel.

- **Mount Scopus**. "The Forum" is where student groups, political alliances, and commercial booths are found. Check out the first floor of the library – a great place for a study group or just a hangout. Ulam 300 (300 Hall) is the only place where some of the classes can take place due to its large size. Go see the amazing views from the nearby amphitheater. Bezalel, the prestigious arts school, is also housed on Mount Scopus.

- **Hadassah Ein Kerem**. Likely the best hospital in the country. And check out the original Chagall windows.

- **Smith Faculty of Agriculture, Food and Environment, Rehovot**. Hebrew U's Koret School of Veterinary Medicine is Israel's sole veterinary school. Rehovot is considered Israel's "Science City." I am proud to say there are two branches of *she codes* in Rehovot too – one at the Weizmann Institute and the other in the Science Park.

Inbar Harush Gity

Inspiration at Hama'alot Theater, Mount Scopus

Inbar Harush Gity *is the CEO of the Tikkun movement. She previously headed the youth development organization Aharai! – Youth Leading Change and the social cohesion movement Pnima Israel. She holds an MA in Public Policy and a BA in Psychology and Biology, both from the Hebrew University.*

We were fifteen, maybe sixteen years old. The Hebrew University seemed like the top of the world to us, especially the law school campus. We climbed up to it from a bus stop that was buried in a dark tunnel. At the top of the long climb, there was a path. Few knew about it, but our friend Ron was crazy about Israel, and he showed us special spots around the whole country. Every Thursday afternoon, he took us to the amphitheater known as Hama'alot Theater. I'll describe the beautiful amphitheater later – but first, a brief introduction.

I grew up in Jerusalem. At first, we lived in the neighborhood of Armon Hanatziv, across from Sur Baher village. Our street, Anusei Mash'had, was full of young families with children of all ages, and we spent long hours riding our bikes outside. Between elementary school and junior high, my parents decided to move to the more sedate Holy Land neighborhood, a new area in western Jerusalem with large and luxurious private homes.

I first heard of Mae Boyar High School, the top school in Jerusalem, when my cousin was accepted there; I worked hard and got in as well. Boyar was everything I hoped for and more. Ambition, high grades, strict teachers, a demanding system – I felt I'd fulfilled my dream. I blossomed there. My friends at Boyar were special, and each one had a unique story. I loved every minute of my experience there.

Throughout our three years at Boyar, we enjoyed endless opportunities, courses, seminars, and fascinating classes. The educational level was outstanding. When I was offered the chance to do a concentration in law at the Hebrew University, I knew I had to take it. It wasn't just the idea of studying law, but that every week on Thursday afternoon, we would travel to the Mount Scopus campus and sit in a lecture hall and learn. We would have a true university experience – not just any university, but the Hebrew University. Again, that flash of personal fulfillment and aspiration to excellence ignited something in me.

To get to the campus, we had to take bus 26A across Jerusalem. Our regular group would meet at the bus stop at Kiryat Hayovel, then spend an hour traveling through Beit Hakerem, Machaneh Yehudah market, the city center, and Bar Ilan Street, until we reached Mount Scopus. The long weekly journey heightened our sense of anticipation and separated our regular life from the university.

On Thursday evenings, the campus was empty of students. We were the only ones there, but we filled the large spaces with our laughter and childhood tales. We'd arrive with half an hour to spare before the lecture began, so we'd race to the amphitheater to catch the sunset. We'd walk for a while and suddenly come upon a panoramic landscape of the Judean Desert. Rows of stairs and stone benches faced the stage. A beautiful stone arch stood at its back edge, and its columns framed five scenes of the desert stretching from the foot of Mount Scopus – a view stunning in its simplicity.

On this exact spot, the Hebrew University was founded. On April 1, 1925, leaders of the Jewish community of the Land of Israel and other dignitaries stood on a wooden platform and delivered speeches: Chief Rabbi of Palestine Avraham Yitzchak Hacohen Kook, Dr. Chaim Weizmann, Lord Arthur Balfour, and poet Hayim Nahman Bialik. The latter declared: "The windows and gates of this house will be open to the four winds, so that it may gather the fine and lofty creations of the human spirit from all times and from all lands." Indeed, the Mount Scopus campus of the Hebrew University of Jerusalem has grown to become one of the most important institutions in Israel and in the world, a focal point of research, study, and knowledge.

Each week we would sit there at dusk and watch the sunset. Ron made crow calls. The conversation that flowed between us was intimate, and we felt connected – to each other, to Israel's land, to our roots, and to our hopes. As Bialik had envisioned, we felt the four winds of the earth and the enormous creative potential within each of us.

After the sun set, we raced back to the dull lecture hall. But the amphitheater had inspired us, a reminder of the magnitude of the opportunity we had been given.

PART VII

TECHNOLOGY, INNOVATION, AND ENTREPRENEURSHIP
The Innovation Nation

Photo: Amit Gabay-Murvitz

Inbal Kreiss is Head of Innovation at the Systems, Missiles, and Space Division of the Israeli Aerospace Industries Ltd. (IAI) and Chairwoman of RAKIA, Israel's Scientific and Technological Mission to the International Space Station. She led the IAI team responsible for Israel's first lunar lander, Beresheet.

Inbal (Biran) Kreiss

Probing the Stars at Mitzpe Ramon Astronomical Observation Center

Mitzpe Ramon in the Negev is one of the best locations in Israel for stargazing and astronomical observation. Strategically located on the northern edge of the Ramon Crater (Makhtesh Ramon), the Mitzpe Ramon planetarium is a thrilling place to visit.

Observing the clear night sky through huge telescopes brings the nebulas, galaxies, and star clusters into sharp relief, providing an unrivalled and uninterrupted viewing experience. The planetarium's majestic location in the middle of the Negev Desert allows the world beyond the horizon to open itself up, revealing an endless, breathtaking composition of celestial life.

The Ramon Crater itself is a unique natural and geological phenomenon. Shaped a bit like an elongated heart, it is twenty-five miles (40 km) long and 1,640 feet (500 m) deep. Its contours and texture are reminiscent of Mars, the planet that enjoys the focus of the international space community, intent on uncovering its secrets and landing a man there in the coming years. The Ramon Crater forms Israel's largest national park (the Ramon Nature Reserve), which ensures its rich variety of flora and fauna is preserved.

I have spent my entire career living, breathing, and dreaming space. As a leader and manager in the Israeli space industry, I bring together scientists, engineers, entrepreneurs, and innovators who collectively make the frontier of space accessible.

Space has had a major impact on modern life. Many technological breakthroughs and remarkable innovations were developed and invented on various space exploration programs. It is hard to imagine our daily life without all the observation, navigation, and communication satellites currently in space. This is why a nation's space capabilities are a measure of its superior power, competency, and technological might.

Israel's space program was established in the 1980s, making it the eighth country in the world to succeed in launching and positioning satellites in space. This triumph brought Israel into the exclusive club of super nations with end-to-end space capabilities and laid the foundation of an enduring heritage that includes novel technological applications developed over the years and competitive products used by the entire international space industry.

As a country forced to deal with security challenges and a shortage of resources, Israel focused on miniaturizing the technology and developing small, lightweight satellites with high resolution, remote sensing, and communication capabilities. Today, Israel is considered a world leader in this industry – a small country with a large relative technological advantage in the field.

Israel's space achievements are perceived as important elements of statehood and indicators of elevated status and power within the international sphere. Israel's space industry highlights its courage to be first, its vision and technological superiority – the unique ingredients of the innovation nation.

Photo: Dr. Avishai Teicher Pikiwiki Israel (CC BY 2.5)

Photo: Heritage Conservation Outside The City Pikiwiki Israel (CC BY 2.5)

I was privileged to lead the spacecraft design and assembly team on Israel's first mission to the moon, Beresheet, in 2019. This exhilarating enterprise started as the private dream of three young entrepreneurs and ended with the entire "innovation nation" following every maneuver all the way to the moon. The Israeli spacecraft was the smallest ever to be sent to the moon and unique in its low redundancy with no back-up systems for its components, making it lighter and cheaper to build than the usual prototype used on space missions.

Beresheet orbited earth in elliptical circuits, traveling a staggering 6.5 million kilometers, the longest distance ever traveled to the moon. Unfortunately, seconds before the end of the landing maneuver, a malfunction in one of the sensors lead to it crashing. But the message was clear: we reached the moon, making Israel the seventh country ever to reach lunar orbit and adding an illustrious chapter to Israel's space history.

At RAKIA, the Scientific and Technological Mission to the International Space Station, of which I was chairwoman, our major objective was to provide a platform for the multitude of Israeli experiments to leverage the lack of gravity and vacuum conditions that exist only in space. These experiments include exploring sources of renewable energy; understanding biological processes for next-generation drugs, vaccines, and medical devices; advancing fiber optics and communications; and even learning how to grow agricultural produce, in preparation for the day we land a man on Mars!

We hope this mission will again capture the imagination of inquisitive young minds and contribute to mankind's growing body of knowledge on the cosmos, thereby positioning Israel as a prime player on the global space map.

When I look up to space and think of Israel's space ecosystem achievements, I can appreciate the profoundness and wisdom of Shimon Peres's vision: Always Dream Big.

Orna Berry

Raising the Scientific Bar in Beer Sheva

During the last sixty years, Beer Sheva's orientation has slowly veered from its original reliance on chemical industries based on regional natural resources. It has shown its advancement in such diverse fields as irrigation and desert colonization (Kibbutz Hatzerim), a significant Israel Air Force base (Hatzerim Base) and the flight academy, and the development of Ben-Gurion University of the Negev, whose presidents over the years have raised the academic base from regional to national research level.

Today, the city, the government, the university, the hospital, the college, real estate developments, multinational industries, and local cultural and technological innovation have all transformed the dusty Ottoman city into a high-quality living and employment option for many. Beer Sheva provides over half a million regional inhabitants services in education and higher education, culture, employment, health, science and technology, commerce and industry, recreation and leisure.

Transportation to the city has become increasingly accessible via train and significant improvements to the regional road system.

The high-tech park established in Beer Sheva – in walking distance from Ben-Gurion University, Soroka Medical Center, the train station, and the forthcoming IDF technology campus – attracts technology companies, including multinational and Israeli tech firms, as well as funds and incubators breeding additional tech start-ups. Israel's National Cyber Directorate has also moved on site. A recent study by Brandeis University has chosen Beer Sheva as one of seven world-leading cities in significant technology-based growth.

Dr. Orna Berry *is a recognized high-tech entrepreneur, scientist, policy maker and industry executive. She is the only woman to have served as Israel's Chief Scientist and Director of the Industrial Research and Development Administration. She is director of technology in the office of the CTO at Google Cloud.*

Artist's conception of the Campus for the Intelligence Professions (courtesy of Shikun & Binui Ltd.)

The city has a long-term plan that includes investments in human capital and advanced educational programs in the school system and in institutions of higher education.

Long-term planning also includes sustainability, ecology, and the development of regional anchors in the fields of tourism, arts, and culture, as well as performing arts events and visual arts exhibitions highlighting original local creation.

The national plan to move IDF technology units includes expanding employment opportunities, new residential quarters, and health and educational infrastructures.

Present-day Beer Sheva inspires meaningful pioneering spirit and significant local pride in its residents, generating a win-win constellation for its local population and employers who have established businesses of all sizes in the city.

We tend to tie culture and history with water and food resources. The biblical town of Beersheba was founded when Abraham and Abimelech settled their differences over a well of water and made a covenant. Its name derives from the terms *be'er* (well) and *shevua* (oath) in the ancient language.

The modern-day city served as an Ottoman administrative center for the benefit of the Bedouin at the outset of the twentieth century. During World War I, the Ottomans built the Hejaz Railway from Damascus to Medina and several branches into modern-day Israel. Beer Sheva was inaugurated in October 1915.

Beer Sheva was liberated from the Ottomans by the British, led by General Allenby, and Australian and New Zealand Army Corps (ANZAC) forces on October 31, 1917. This was the last successful cavalry charge in British military history, and it was followed by the Balfour Declaration announcing support for the establishment of a "national home for the Jewish people" on November 2, 1917, prior to the completion of the British conquest of then Palestine.

On the edge of Beer Sheva's Old City is the Beersheba War Cemetery, containing the graves of soldiers from Australia, New Zealand, and Great Britain. The Australian Jewish community and the city of Beer Sheva have built a memorial park in honor of the fallen.

In 1948, during the Israeli War of Independence, David Ben-Gurion approved the conquest of Beer Sheva as proposed by Yigal Alon in a strategic operation that freed the Negev as a whole.

The 1949 Armistice Agreements, following the conclusion of the war, formally granted Beer Sheva to Israel. The town was then transformed into a prominent Israeli city. Beer Sheva was deemed strategically important due to its location, with a reliable water supply and at a major crossroads to the Negev.

Present-day Beer Sheva maintains the historic status of a regional metropolitan center, while also coming up as a global leader in multiple fields of civic achievement.

Hillel Fuld

Old Meets New at First Station

Hillel Fuld is a global speaker, tech columnist, and start-up marketing advisor who has been dubbed by Forbes "the man transforming start-up nation to scale up nation."

I was born and raised in New York, then moved to Israel with my family at the age of fifteen. My parents were and are hardcore Zionists who got on a plane at their first opportunity to come home to the Land of Israel.

I grew up with the love of Israel running through my veins. Like many *olim* (immigrants to Israel), we moved to Jerusalem (specifically, the Baka area). While the transition from New York to Jerusalem involved extreme culture shock, one thing that struck me about living in Israel was the juxtaposition or the combination of old and new, of past and future, of tradition and innovation.

I believe that no place illustrates that bridge between the past and the future better than the First Station in Jerusalem.

The First Station is situated only minutes away from the Old City of Jerusalem, and in the other direction, only a few minutes from the center of town.

You will find daily shows and plays in the First Station, as well as some of the best restaurants in the city. Additionally, you will find Segway tours, souvenir shops, and endless booths of independent artists selling their work. Some leading venture capital firms are also located in the station, including Jerusalem Venture Partners and Ourcrowd. Not only is JVP located in the station, but many of its portfolio companies have set up shop there as well. And all of this is located in a place that used to be a train station.

The vibe in the First Station is truly unique, and it is, in my opinion, the perfect representation of what Israel is, the place where the past and future meet.

As someone fortunate enough to work in what has become one of the world's leading innovation ecosystems, I am able to meet some of the most fascinating and brilliant entrepreneurs in the world, almost on a daily basis. These entrepreneurs all have one thing in common: they are building the future.

However, let's not forget what David Ben-Gurion presented in the United Nations as the justification for the return of the Jewish people to the Land of Israel. He showed the Hebrew Bible. So while Israeli founders are building the future using artificial intelligence, machine learning, and so many more technological breakthroughs, we are only here in the Land of Israel because of the past. What brought us back here after thousands of years of exile is our tradition. That is the unique nature of the modern State of Israel.

Anyone who knows anything about technology hears "Israel" and thinks of the book *Start-Up Nation*, which was written over a decade ago to explain how Israel – a country smaller than New Jersey in one of the most unstable regions on earth – has become a leading technology superpower in less than eighty years.

While tech development is found in many cities across Israel – including Tel Aviv, Herzliya, Caesarea, Haifa, and many more –an incredible amount of technology is being developed right here in the capital of Israel, Jerusalem. Some of the biggest Israeli success stories in the technology sector have taken place in Jerusalem. NDS, a Jerusalem-based company, was acquired by Cisco for $5 billion, for example.

One cannot talk about success stories in Israeli tech without mentioning the $15.2 billion acquisition of Mobileye by Intel. Mobileye is of course a Jerusalem-based company as well. In fact, Professor Amnon Shaashua, the CEO and founder of Mobileye (and the person I call "the Elon Musk of Israel"), lives right outside of Jerusalem. I was fortunate to ride in the next-generation Mobileye autonomous vehicle from his house to Mobileye HQ in Jerusalem. Never did I feel more in the future than that morning.

Jerusalem is one of the fastest-growing technology hubs worldwide, but never forget that it is also the city that is holy to three major religions and has historical sites from thousands of years ago, including of course the Western Wall and the Temple Mount.

The First Station has all of this. A ten-minute walk from the First Station of Jerusalem and you find yourself praying at the Western Wall, but if you choose to walk in the opposite direction, those

same ten minutes will lead you to the center of town, where you can experience all the rich culture the city has to offer and the many start-up companies that have set their roots in the historic city of Jerusalem. The First Station has all of this. A ten-minute walk from the First Station of Jerusalem and you find yourself praying at the Western Wall, but if you choose to walk in the opposite direction, those same ten minutes will lead you to the center of town, where you can experience all the rich culture the city has to offer and the many start-up companies that have set their roots in the historic city of Jerusalem.

Moshe Friedman

Building Bridges at KamaTech Innovation Center, Bnei Brak

The KamaTech Innovation Center sits at the top of BSR Tower 4 in the Bnei Brak Business Center, strategically located on the border between Bnei Brak and Ramat Gan.

KamaTech's balcony offers a panoramic view of central Israel. To the west, we can see the Yarkon Park, the beaches of Tel Aviv, Jaffa Port, and the Israel Diamond Exchange in Ramat Gan. To the north Tel Aviv University, Herzliya, and the Sharon area are visible. To the south, Givatayim stands in the distance, while up close is Bnei Brak, with its plethora of yeshivas and synagogues. The ornate Ponevezh Yeshiva adorns a hilltop across from us, while to the east are Giv'at Shmuel, Bar-Ilan University, Petach Tikvah, the Atidim Hi-Tech Park, and Rosh Ha'ayin. Further east sprawl the rolling hills of Judea and Samaria.

From inside the KamaTech Innovation Center, we realize just how small Israel really is. We live so close to one another that we must be unified – divisiveness is simply not an option. This is why my partners and I established the center. We called the initial iteration of KamaTech Ampersand – the symbol of connection – because it's a place for connecting communities, linking entrepreneurs and building bridges between people.

The ultra-Orthodox public in Israel today numbers about one million, approximately 12 percent of Israel's population and its fastest-growing sector. Some 25 percent of Israeli children are ultra-Orthodox. But in the high-tech workforce, ultra-Orthodox members comprise less than 3 percent. This represents a sizeable challenge but also an enormous opportunity for Israel's economy and future as the "start-up nation." The ultra-Orthodox public has untapped

Moshe Friedman is an ultra-Orthodox entrepreneur who has founded various initiatives to integrate ultra-Orthodox people into the high-tech workforce, including KamaTech, TicTech, and the I2A Venture Capital Fund.

reserves of talent and creativity, and brilliant, sharp minds that can contribute to high-tech innovation. Joining these reserves to Israel's economy will help it make the leap into the future.

Bnei Brak is considered the capital of the ultra-Orthodox world. Most of the leading ultra-Orthodox rabbis and yeshivas are located there. It is home to a significant number of great Torah scholars and some of the most important institutions of Torah study in the Jewish world. At the same time, Bnei Brak has the highest population density and the lowest socioeconomic level in Israel. It may be poor in material assets, but it is rich in spiritual achievement. It has the lowest crime rate and the highest life expectancy in Israel. In surveys and studies, its residents report a very high level of happiness. They live long lives and are content with their lot.

The KamaTech Innovation Center coworking space is located at the heart of Bnei Brak's business hub. Our center was constructed in cooperation with major high-tech companies and furnished with the most advanced technological equipment. It provides a space for ultra-Orthodox start-ups and talented, ambitious ultra-Orthodox innovators. These include programmers, engineers, designers, entrepreneurs, and businesspeople. The center has classrooms where courses and professional training sessions are given on a variety of topics, including technology, design, marketing, advertising, and entrepreneurship. There are also halls for events and conferences, meeting rooms, offices, and workstations. The balcony has become a popular space for hosting events.

In addition to encouraging technological progress, the center was built to provide a solution for the ultra-Orthodox population to be able to work according to the halachic laws of separation between men and women. There are separate spaces for men and women to work and study. There are also shared public spaces for meetings, a *mehadrin* (most stringently kosher) cafeteria, and a synagogue for services and Torah classes. In a celebration of ultra-Orthodox identity, the entrepreneurs at the center maintain pride in their distinctive religious character while simultaneously joining the forefront of technological achievement.

The center represents a beacon of innovation and entrepreneurship within the ultra-Orthodox community. Each day, hundreds of men and women from the community attend conferences and events, including hackathons, job fairs, lectures, meetups, workshops, and meetings. Hundreds of groups visit the center each year for a firsthand look at ultra-Orthodox high tech in creation. A long list of investors, managers, and entrepreneurs also visit to develop business connections and build bridges between the ultra-Orthodox and the broader Israeli high-tech community. Guests from Israel and abroad help transform the center into a focal point for global cooperative ventures.

Israel's future is located at the intersection of these connections, and technology is an amazing tool for building bridges. I invite you to visit the KamaTech Innovation Center, to see how this future is happening today – *baruch Hashem* (thank God)!

Gil Shwed

Tel Aviv
A Concept City

Tel Aviv is not just a city. For me, Tel Aviv represents the new Israel, or as the eighties slogan that was adopted to describe it goes, it is "the city that never sleeps."

Israel's modern history embodies innovation – the creation of something new. On the one hand, Israel is very much connected to its profound past (see Jerusalem, a city I love and where I was born and raised), rooted to its soil (see our blooming agriculture in the Negev and the Galilee), and at the same time always looking to innovate and create an even better future.

Tel Aviv is the capital of Israel's connection to the future, in culture and art, security and economy, and in recent years, on the high-tech scene.

In the 2000s, Israel became known as the "start-up nation," the epicenter of technology. Technology is a global field that requires access to the world, and Tel Aviv quickly delivered on that mission with hundreds of start-ups that capitalize on the openness of the city, working in a cosmopolitan world.

The talent that nurtures this industry is cultivated and grown all over Israel. It is educated in our universities and graduated from the different units of our army, but at a certain point, all the talent comes to Tel Aviv to master the world of technology and work in the best tech companies out there.

In 1993, when I established Check Point Software Technologies (today Israel's largest tech company and a world leader in cybersecurity), I debated whether I should base the company in Jerusalem, my hometown. I decided that Tel Aviv was the right city, with access to the right

Gil Shwed is the cofounder and CEO of Check Point Software Technologies Ltd., one of Israel's largest technology companies and the world's largest pure-play cybersecurity company. He is considered the inventor of the modern Firewall and one of the world's most experienced experts in cybersecurity.

Photos: Gil Shwed

talent. Its central location makes it accessible to commuters from all over the country, and people from all over the world want to come and visit. Almost thirty years later, Tel Aviv has surely delivered on that promise. Tel Aviv symbolizes many of Israel's greatest virtues, and we take special pride in the fact that it has become a global symbol of high tech and especially cybersecurity.

To me, Tel Aviv is far more than a high-tech city. It is the modern center of Israel. It is a center of business and culture, filled with theaters (Habima National Theater, the Cameri Theater, Beit Lessin Theater, Gesher Theater, Hasimta Theater, and the Jaffa Theater). It is also the hometown of the Israel Philharmonic and home to many large and small museums such as the Tel Aviv Museum of Art, the MUZA – Eretz Israel Museum, and ANU – Museum of the Jewish People, just to name a few. Tel Aviv is also a culinary pearl, with hundreds of cafés, bars, and restaurants open around the clock.

Tel Aviv is a synonym for innovation, liberalism, freedom, and a vibrant connection to the world. It has become a model for many others – both in Israel and abroad. Restaurant owners in Israel's north often try to emulate the atmosphere of Tel Aviv. High-tech hubs in the south are compared to the ones in Tel Aviv. This is the actual definition of leadership – setting a model for an innovative, modern vision others want to follow. Not everybody needs to be in Tel Aviv, but many want to be like it.

To me, Tel Aviv's concept defines the Israeli spirit: making wonders out of what you're given, out-of-the-box innovation, and a healthy drive to expand beyond existing boundaries. It may not be home for everyone, but every visitor feels most welcome upon arrival. Tel Aviv's concept is the beating heart of an amazing nation, and I'm sure that its future holds even greater promise.

Adi Soffer Teeni

My Corner of Rothschild Boulevard, Tel Aviv

Adi Soffer Teeni is the Vice President and General Manager of Meta (formerly Facebook) Israel.

On the corner of Rothschild Boulevard and Nachlat Binyamin, at the heart of Tel Aviv, we opened our FB TLV office in 2014.

When our global teams called to ask me where I thought we should set up our offices, it took me about two seconds to say it absolutely has to be Rothschild – not just because of the incredible views of the city or how close we were to our clients and partners, but mainly because I wanted us to start FB's story in the "start-up nation" in the exact same place where the story of modern-day Israel began.

We often talk about Israel as the start-up nation, because of the incredible success of the tech industry in the country over the years. But the truth is, Israel itself is something of a start-up.

A country founded against all odds, aiming to solve an age-old problem, with incredibly limited natural resources, fueled by big dreams, deep faith, and a very stubborn group of people who brought their best talents and hard work to build something out of nothing.

And this is not just because of the Israeli entrepreneurial mindset or because of our passion, but rather because we just had no other choice. They say the person who invented the wheel wasn't necessarily the smartest, but just the one who really needed a wheel. And back then, in the late 1940s, as a people that had no other choice and really needed that wheel, we had to get creative in building it.

But even before there was Israel, Rothschild is where the story of Tel Aviv began. The first Hebrew city was founded in 1909, when a group of sixty-six Jewish families gathered on the sand dunes that would later become this beautiful boulevard and decided to build a new city. Among those families who each got a piece of land were my great-grandparents, who became founders of the newborn city.

Over the decades to come, these families have turned Tel Aviv from a neighborhood into a city, building streets and roads, schools and public institutions, and slowly making Tel Aviv the cultural center of the soon-to-be Jewish state. Tel Aviv also became a financial hub, home to new businesses, factories, and shopping centers.

And then came the first Israeli entrepreneur and founder, David Ben-Gurion, who saw a problem that needed to be solved, used all the resources he could find, and started growing this incredible start-up. He focused on building more cities and towns, establishing public institutions, harnessing technology to overcome the lack of natural resources, and finding investors who were willing to take a bet and support this crazy dream of building a home for the Jewish people in Israel.

And then, on May 14, 1948, eight hours before the British Mandate over the land was about to end, and while Jerusalem was under siege by Arab forces, David Ben-Gurion gathered his cabinet in Tel Aviv to declare the establishment of the State of Israel. The ceremony was held in secret with only a small crowd, in the former house of Meir Dizengoff, the first mayor of Tel Aviv. That house, at 16 Rothschild Boulevard, only a few buildings down from our offices, is today Israel's Independence Hall.

To me, Rothschild Boulevard tells the full story of the start-up nation. From the birthplace of a disruptive idea of a state to the heart of the city with the most start-ups per capita, every corner of this street tells a piece of history, every building a testament to how far we've come.

On one hand, this is where Israel's traditional industries began to build, where the first banks opened, where retail and commerce thrived, where our economy was founded. And on the other hand, this street houses some of the most innovative, cutting-edge, and successful Israeli start-ups today. The same street that Meir Dizengoff and David Ben-Gurion walked is now home to so many new entrepreneurs, using that same innovative mindset to find creative solutions to new challenges.

If you asked me what I'm most passionate about, or what I love most, I'd say the following three things: my family, Israel, and the Israeli tech ecosystem. To me, Rothschild Boulevard is where all three of them meet, which makes it my absolute favorite place in Israel, and I feel so privileged to get to walk through it every single day.

Itay Pincas *has been a tech entrepreneur since he was twelve and has developed more than thirty mobile apps. He is a regular lecturer and advisor on designing digital products aimed at Gen Z. He has been recognized as a promising leader by Forbes' 30 Under 30 list. He was born in 2001.*

Itay Pincas

Innovation in Tel Aviv

Whenever I contemplate how Israel has become a global technological and entrepreneurial powerhouse in such a short period of time, I can't help but think of the major role the city of Tel Aviv-Jaffa has played in bringing us to this point.

Once a Jewish suburb of the ancient Mediterranean port of Jaffa, the modern city of Tel Aviv has developed into one of the most important economic and cultural centers in Israel. Tel Aviv is home to most of the headquarters of Israel's large corporations, as well as banks, foreign embassies, and Israel's stock exchange, not to mention a staggering number of start-ups. Often called "the city that never sleeps," Tel Aviv has had an immensely significant influence on Israel's position as the "start-up nation."

At the age of twelve, I released my first app on the App Store. I dreamed of becoming a competent developer and came to the conclusion that I needed a mentor. I was immediately advised to look in Tel Aviv, where I was told I would find new start-ups forming on a "daily basis" by extremely passionate people. I found countless lovely, intelligent, and helpful people, through meet-ups and conferences across the city, who were incredibly generous with their time and willingness to assist me in person.

That's when I first fell in love with the city of Tel Aviv – and in particular, with the people who live and work there. The characteristic mixture of the typical Israeli chutzpah along with unbounded patience and a willingness to help others, despite being busy and preoccupied with one's own ventures, is a foundation stone of Israel's culture. Specifically, it is a major factor in Israel's entrepreneurial success and continues to help us solve some of the world's problems.

One of the city's most notable initiatives aimed at solving some key worldwide challenges is the so called "hackathon." These take place regularly around the city and typically involve several teams who work together with a vision of

solving a challenge in a given field (such as healthcare), producing a proof of concept on a tight schedule.

When I was fourteen years old, I decided to give it a shot. I signed up for a hackathon aimed at solving the growing "driving under the influence" issue among teenagers. After three weeks and countless slices of pizza, my team and I won the competition. As excited as I was about the triumph, what really made me happy was the realization that these sorts of activities, which very much define the city's high-tech culture, are open and available to all. No matter your age, gender, or ethnicity, if you're willing to work hard and cooperate with others toward building a better future and making technology accessible globally, you couldn't be more welcomed in this city.

In recent years, Tel Aviv has become a magnet for global economic activities and a target for many overseas delegations looking to learn from the locals, so that their communities can attain the same level of creativity. Unsurprisingly, many large tech firms have selected Tel Aviv as their R&D headquarters.

One of my most memorable moments in the city was when I had the honor of meeting the executive team of Huawei at the Royal Beach Hotel in Tel Aviv. While speaking to some of the executives from the Chinese tech giants, I couldn't help but think of how privileged we are as a nation to have managed to build such a vibrant, thriving, and embracing culture that has produced so many breakthroughs. But the true privilege, I believe, lies in our capacity for sharing that knowledge with others and introducing ourselves to more mature countries such as China that are so keen to learn from us. It struck me that we shouldn't take this for granted.

Although there are numerous places in the city that I'd recommend visiting, I wouldn't do it justice if I were to neglect the very special Peres Center for Peace and Innovation. Located on the shores of the Old City of Jaffa, it beautifully portrays the story of how Israel came to be a true pioneer.

As the final exhibit of the Peres Center suggests, we should always look to the future and be inspired by the number of problems yet to be solved, by the challenges awaiting humanity, in the years and decades to come. We should all be seeking new knowledge and experience, just like the late Shimon Peres, when he invited me to his office just so he could be taught how to use Snapchat at the ripe age of ninety-three! If Mr. Peres was willing to learn something so new, so unfamiliar to him at such an age, what excuse do we have not to follow his lead?

Chemi Peres is a venture capital and innovation pioneer and serves as the Chairman of the Board of Directors of the Peres Center for Peace and Innovation, Israel's leading nonprofit organization, established in 1996 by his late father, Israel's ninth President and former Prime Minister Shimon Peres.

Chemi Peres

The Peres Center for Peace and Innovation

The Peres Center for Peace and Innovation is located in a breathtakingly beautiful building in the heart of the Ajami neighborhood on the shores of Old Jaffa. This neighborhood is in the southern region of the Tel Aviv-Jaffa municipality and is home to both Jews and Arabs.

The Peres Center building was designed by renowned Italian architect Massimiliano Fuksas and constructed in close cooperation with Israeli architect Yoav Messer. The long, rectangular structure faces west to the sea and the red sunsets of Jaffa. The façade is glass, while the other sides are formed of layers of green-tinted concrete and glass. This permits the building to absorb light and heat throughout the day, while at night it illuminates the surrounding area. To me, the concrete layers symbolize the rich history of the Land of Israel, while the glass façade integrates future possibilities. The changing forms of the concrete slabs recall the dynamic movement of breaking waves, drawing the blue waves of the Mediterranean Sea into the structure.

Since its founding in 1996, the Peres Center for Peace and Innovation has worked to create ties among people who together attempt to forge a new future of coexistence. The Peres Center focuses on inspiring us to create a better tomorrow by designing a new future for us all. As Shimon Peres, the center's founder and ninth president of the State of Israel, often said, "We can't change the past – but we can shape the future." He aimed this vision at tomorrow's youth, our future generation of leaders, saying, "Now it's your turn." He believed in the enormous potential of each and every member of our society. With faith and great optimism, we can reach our dreams. We can create a reality in which we stride forward together into a new age of prosperity and growth, a life of peace and security – for Jews and Arabs, secular and religious, Israelis and citizens of the neighboring states.

The Peres Center's programs focus on creating bridges for coexistence by initiating projects in a wide range of fields, including agriculture and environment, medicine, culture, and sports. Each project involves youth, Jews, Arabs, Israelis,

The Peres Center, looking to the south with the city of Bat Yam on the horizon

and Palestinians. In recent years, the Peres Center has begun to launch projects in the fields of innovation and entrepreneurship. In late 2018, the center introduced a new visitors' center to inspire and educate visitors on the power of innovation and entrepreneurship and to share with them the Israeli journey of the last hundred years.

The visitors' center presents Shimon Peres's vision of peace and innovation – a journey from an old world into the new age. In the old world, as Peres liked to say, the power of a society depended on the land where it settled and the richness of its natural resources. In order to grow, the world's peoples fought over land and resources, bloodying human history with wars of occupation, killing, and enslavement.

But in the new age, as Peres envisioned, the source of power lies in knowledge and science, innovation and entrepreneurship – the power of the mind. We can imagine and create a better world – we can dream and implement.

Human societies have built nations, defined borders, and created military forces, aiming to defend their property and gain power by conquering more land. In this old worldview, the growth of one nation is at the expense of its neighbors. But now, Peres declared, we are at the gateway to a new era. For the first time in human history, we have the opportunity to attain new heights. Through innovation and entrepreneurship, we can grow and prosper without harming others. We can create a world in which no one loses – a world without war or killing.

The Peres Center for Peace and Innovation portrays the inspiring life and legacy of Shimon Peres, which is intertwined with the birth and growth of the State of Israel. Israel aims to push forward into this new age from within a region that remains mired in the old world of war, hatred, and violence.

Israel is the first state in the region that was built with the strength of pioneers, entrepreneurs, innovators, and inventors. During the initial period of settlement and building the state, Israel focused on the fields of agriculture, water, and energy. Out of necessity, we developed technologies for desalinating seawater into fresh water and for creating a modern water system. We developed drip irrigation technology to enable settlement and agriculture in dry, infertile regions.

Because we live in such a small land, we have no surrounding mountain ranges or broad rivers that can protect us from an attacker. So we must use science and technology to defend ourselves. Through science and technology and daring innovation, we built defensive walls around our tiny country – from construction of the nuclear reactor in Dimona to establishment of the Israel Aerospace Industries and defense industry. We crossed the frontier of space. We developed missiles as a defensive umbrella, and we built a wall of cyber defense.

We followed the same course with our economy. Because our state is small, we have few natural resources. In addition, we live on a virtual island surrounded by hostile states. So we cannot create a strong economy by ourselves. We must work with the world beyond and export products and services based on science and technology.

This is the story of the birth of the "innovation nation." First, we invited global companies to establish research and development centers in Israel. They came by the dozens and then by the hundreds. At the same time, we offered incentives to bright youth to establish homegrown Israeli start-ups. We began with a few – today there are thousands.

Now we must continue this journey into the new age. We must untether ourselves from the world of war over land as quickly as possible and enter the age of human cooperation. Together we can face the dangers that have replaced the wars of the

Various activities at the Peres Center

past. We can work to prevent extreme climate change, collaborate to block contagious pandemics such as COVID-19, deal with cyber and physical terrorism, stabilize the global economy that affects all our lives, and solve the problem of refugees who flee cruel, old-world states for safe borders.

I invite you to take a tour of the Peres Center. We begin at the visitors' center entry hall, which aims to inspire each and every youth and visitor by presenting the power of technology and innovation coupled with visionary entrepreneurship to improve the world. The center portrays a number of Israeli innovations that improve the lives of millions of people around the world. Here you will meet some of the best Israeli innovators, inventors, and entrepreneurs, who serve as examples of human genius. They dream, think, act, and realize their dreams. They have dedicated their lives to creating a better, safer society. They are scientists and researchers, social entrepreneurs, leaders of major technology companies, men and women, Jews and Arabs, youth and seniors, from all sectors of Israeli society.

The building's second level, the history gallery, describes the path we have taken and on which we continue. The story begins in the pre-state days and continues to present times. It is a story of constant innovation. This level features one hundred milestones, each marking a significant inspirational moment in the formation of the "start-up nation."

Level three, the future level, describes in a time capsule the challenges to humanity in the next two decades and the inherent possibilities for innovation.

The tour ends with a peek into the contemporary Innovation Gallery, where we see what is being done in Israel here and now, featuring dozens of groundbreaking start-up companies that aim to improve the world with life-changing developments.

We conclude our tour of the Peres Center with the words of our founder, President Shimon Peres: "Looking around at the wonderful reality of Israel and our achievements in the first seventy years of independence, and looking back at the early days of the state – I realize that we should have dreamed more. Don't hold back on dreams. Don't be afraid. Keep dreaming, and always dream big."

Chemi Peres and Ilan Greenfield

Acknowledgments

Creating a book like *My Israel* with seventy busy contributors is no easy task. When we started implementing our concept of the book, our first task was to come up with a list of our partners and contributors.

We both went to school together and were neighbors. We both served in the IDF. We have been around Israel and know the land, the political scene, the business environment, and academia. We are also both engaged in the nonprofit world in Israel.

During this process, we were fortunate to have many professionals, friends, and peers who loved the concept and did everything they could to assist us in accomplishing the task of publishing *My Israel*. We would like to take this opportunity to show them our deep appreciation for the labor of love that they invested so we could publish this special book.

Our thanks to Cynthia Diaz at Pitango Venture Capital and Liat (Greenfield) Azar at Gefen Publishing House who started from scratch and gathered all the articles, devoting hours of detailed work.

To the Gefen staff, especially our senior editor, Kezia Raffel Pride, who guided us through and made sure every word was in the right place, and Valeria Bauer, our project manager, who oversaw the process and ensured we had all the pieces put together.

To Shira Rivelis for her important input, writings, and ideas, and to Sharonna Karni Cohen – both helped us by referring writers and conducting interviews on our behalf. A special thank-you to Inbal Arieli, who introduced both Shira and Sharonna to us. All three became contributors to this book as well.

We would like to specially thank Jaki Levi, the designer.

Many talented photographers assisted us in selecting the beautiful photos of locations around the country. Thanks to Itai Bardov, Ziv Koren, Moses Pini Siluk, Dror Gabay, Gil Shwed with the help of Gil Messing at Checkpoint, Amichay Zini, Amit Gabay-Murvitz, and Shiran Halimi. There were no easy choices given the beautiful images we have seen.

There must be many more who have assisted us along this journey. Thanks to all of you, we have *My Israel*.

Last but not least, we thank our wives, Gila and Caryn, and our entire families for their loving support of the project.

May the country we all love so much always be *our Israel* – for all of us and for future generations – and may we inhabit the land together in love, solidarity, and mutual respect.

Chemi Peres and Ilan Greenfield

March 2023, Ra'anana and Kfar Adumim, Israel

Index of Contributors

Alshekh, Maysa Hazabi	92	Gold-Zamir, Dr. Yael	122	Rabinovitch, Rabbi Shmuel	119
Altschuler, Adi	72	Greenfield, Murray	13	Radinsky, Kira	22
Arad, Yael	175	Harari, Brig. Gen. (Ret.) Dani	69	Rado, Hana	97
Argov, Gideon	25	Hare-Cohen, Sharon	20	Rahav-Meir, Sivan	64
Arieli, Inbal	149	Hasson, Brig. Gen. (Ret.) Hasson	10	Rivelis, Shira	144
Ariely, Prof. Dan	50	Klein, Achiya	30	Samuels, Kalman	106
Avni, Aki	154	Klinger, Tchia Efron	58	Satchi-Fainaro, Prof. Ronit	172
Bar-Or, Rabbi Mordechai	127	Kolber, Jonathan	16	Schoenberg, Ido, and Phyllis Gotlib	77
Beck, Dr. Avital	147	Kolitz, Dr. Tamara	136	Shaffir, Stav	53
Beer, Eli	2	Kreiss, Inbal (Biran)	188	Sharon, Gilad	74
Ben-Ami, Lili	27	Kremer, Avichai (Avi)	163	Shilon, Ziv	4
Berry, Orna	191	Lau, Rabbi Binyamin	125	Shwed, Gil	201
Besnainou, Pierre	36	Levenberg, Prof. Shulamit	166	Stibbe, Eytan	101
Bloch, Dr. Aliza	66	Lichtenstein, Chen	60	Strauss, Ofra	81
Broza, David	141	Low, Joey	99	Suchard, Lior	131
Cohen, Itai	7	Machluf, Prof. Marcelle	62	Tashome-Katz, Yuvi	104
Cohen, Sharonna Karni	134	Nahmias-Verbin, Ayelet	38	Teeni, Adi Soffer	203
Eizenkot, Lt. Gen. Gadi	45	Natour-Hafi, Shirin	178	Telhami, Imad	84
Engel, Jossef Avi Yair "Jucha"	41	Nevzlin, Irina	110	Yaari, Sivan	64
Friedman, Moshe	197	Ohana, Tal	56	Zafrir, Nadav	33
Fuld, Hillel	193	Peres, Chemi	158, 208	Zaher, Julia	156
Gadiesh, Orit	151	Peretz, Miriam	47	Ze'evi, Arik	169
Gershony, Noam	89	Pincas, Itay	206		
Gity, Inbar Harush	184	Polachek, Ruth	180		

Chemi Peres

About the Compiler

Chemi Peres is one of Israel's foremost venture capital and innovation pioneers, serving as Managing Partner and cofounder of Pitango Venture Capital, Israel's leading venture capital group, with a portfolio of some three hundred high-tech start-ups and enterprises with global operations. Mr. Peres, with a wealth of experience, is an integral part of the thriving Israeli innovation scene and a key player on the global entrepreneurial stage. Mr. Peres serves on the boards of directors of various Pitango portfolio companies, including Taboola (NASDAQ:TBLA), Via Transportation, Masterschool, Duda, and more. He also serves on the board of directors of Teva Pharmaceuticals, (NYSE:TEVA), the world's largest generic drug supplier.

Chemi is the Chairman of the Board of Directors of the Peres Center for Peace and Innovation, Israel's leading nonprofit organization, established in 1996 by his late father Israel's ninth President and former Prime Minister Shimon Peres.

Mr. Peres is active in other nonprofit organizations and impact investment platforms.

Mr. Peres holds a BSc in industrial engineering and management and an MBA from Tel Aviv University. He served as a pilot in the Israeli Air Force (IAF).

Chemi is married to Gila. They have three children (Nadav, Guy, and Yael) and two granddaughters (Tamar and Zohar) and live in Ra'anana, Israel.

Ilan Greenfield

About the Compiler

Ilan Greenfield is one of Israel's leading publishers. Since 1982, he has been the owner and CEO of Gefen Publishing House, a privately owned publishing house founded by his parents, Hana Greenfield, z"l, and Murray Greenfield.

Ilan served as treasurer of Telem, the Movement for Zionist Fulfilment. He is a licensed tour guide in Israel and is also a founder of the Ein Prat Leadership Academy, on whose board of directors he has served since its founding in 2001.

Ilan serves as a Vice President at NewsRael, a unique twenty-four seven Israel news app founded in 2020.

Greenfield was chosen by the *Algemeiner* as one of the Top 100 People Positively Influencing Jewish Life, 2022.

A marathon runner, Ilan is married to Caryn. They have four children (Yael, Binyamin Liat, and Maayan) and so far six grandsons (Noam, Shachar, Gilad, Yiftach, Avner, and Hadar) and one granddaughter (Roni) and live in Kfar Adumim, Israel.